ASSIGNMENTS ACROSS THE CURRICULUM

T0336285

ASSIGNMENTS ACROSS THE CURRICULUM

A National Study of College Writing

DAN MELZER

UTAH STATE UNIVERSITY PRESS
Logan

© 2014 by the University Press of Colorado
Published by Utah State University Press

An imprint of University Press of Colorado
5589 Arapahoe Avenue, Suite 206C
Boulder, Colorado 80303

 The University Press of Colorado is a proud member of
The Association of American University Presses.

The University Press of Colorado is a cooperative publishing enterprise supported, in part, by Adams State University, Colorado State University, Fort
Lewis College, Metropolitan State University of Denver, Regis University,
University of Colorado, University of Northern Colorado, Utah State University, and Western State Colorado University.

ISBN: 978-0-87421-939-5 (paperback)
ISBN: 978-0-87421-940-1 (ebook)

Library of Congress Cataloging-in-Publication Data

Melzer, Dan.
  Assignments across the curriculum : a national study of college writing / Dan
Melzer.
      pages cm
   ISBN 978-0-87421-939-5 (paperback) — ISBN 978-0-87421-940-1 (ebook)
 1. English language—Rhetoric—Study and teaching. 2. Report writing—
Study and teaching. I. Title.
   PE1404.M448 2014
   808'.042071173—dc23
                                    2013048380

Cover illustration © Andresr/Shutterstock.com

CONTENTS

ASSIGNMENTS ACROSS THE CURRICULUM

1

A PANORAMIC VIEW OF COLLEGE WRITING

In "The Future of Writing Across the Curriculum: Consensus and Research," Chris Anson (1993) traces the history of research in Writing Across the Curriculum (WAC), from early evidence of writing across disciplines that was mostly anecdotal to current research that emphasizes case study and ethnographic methods. Anson approves of the recent qualitative WAC research that has moved beyond "anecdotes, testimonies, and reports from colleagues," but he also calls for more large-scale research into disciplinary writing (xvi). Elsewhere Anson (1988) has argued for "larger scale measures of belief and practice" (24) that will explore questions such as, "What does it mean to write in a particular academic discipline? How do the criteria for good writing differ among diverse disciplines? What sorts of instructional beliefs about writing do scholars in different academic disciplines hold?" (3).

Some of the richest WAC research exploring Anson's questions has come from ethnographic studies of students writing in a course or courses, such as Anne Herrington's (1985) "Writing in Academic Settings: A Study of the Contexts for Writing in Two College Chemical Engineering Classes," Lucille Parkinson McCarthy's (1987) "A Stranger in Strange Lands," and McCarthy and Barbara Walvoord's *Thinking and Writing in College* (Walvoord and McCarthy 1991). Even more extensive are recent longitudinal studies of college student writers, such as Marilyn Sternglass's (1997) *Time to Know Them*, Anne Herrington and Marcia Curtis's *Persons in Process* (Herrington and Curtis 2000), Lee Ann Caroll's (2002) *Rehearsing New Roles*,

DOI: 10.7330/9780874219401.c001

Anne Beaufort's (2007) *College Writing and Beyond*, and studies conducted by Nancy Sommers and Laura Saltz at Harvard (Sommers and Saltz 2004) and Jenn Fishman et al. (2005) at Stanford. These researchers followed a student or a group of students from their first year of college to graduation and beyond, using ethnographic methods to discuss everything from instructors' expectations for writing and students' writing processes, to relationships between composing and contextual factors such as race, class, and gender.

Ethnographic research into writing in the disciplines, however, hasn't provided a large-scale look at college writing in the United States. Other than a handful of researchers in the 1980s who conducted surveys or collected undergraduate assignments from faculty at a single institution or a small group of institutions (Bridgeman and Carlson 1984; Eblen 1983; Harris and Hult 1985; Horowitz 1986; Rose 1983), large-scale research into college writing that could serve as a complement to naturalistic studies has been rare in the field of composition. James Britton and his research team's seminal study of 2,122 pieces of student writing from sixty-five British secondary schools, reported in *The Development of Writing Abilities (11–18)*, has yet to be replicated at the college level (Britton et al. 1975). To use a film analogy, from the outstanding work of ethnographers of writing in the disciplines we have the close-up shot (studies of students' writing in a class or classes in the disciplines) and the mid-range shot (longitudinal studies at single institutions). What this book attempts to provide is the shot that has been neglected in composition research—the panorama.

Through a study of 2,101 writing assignments across disciplines in 100 American postsecondary institutions, I reveal patterns in the rhetorical situations, genres, and discourse communities of college writing that complement, confirm, and sometimes complicate the data from ethnographic research. Although this study sacrifices the pedagogical context and "thick description" (Geertz 1973) of ethnographic research (the panoramic view by its nature does not capture the level of detail of the close up shot), it provides what ethnographic research cannot—the shot that pans wide enough that larger patterns in the landscape are revealed. These larger patterns concerning college writing in the United States are of interest to WAC practitioners working with faculty across disciplines, writing center coordinators and tutors working with students who bring assignments to their writing centers from a variety of fields, composition program administrators and first-year writing instructors who are interested in preparing students for college writing, and high school teachers looking to create a bridge between high school and college writing. In order to explore disciplinary writing on a larger scale than ethnography, and provide a view of the kinds of patterns in the landscape that will have relevance to all of these various stakeholders in academic literacies, I collected and analyzed one of the fundamental pieces of classroom discourse: writing assignments.

WHAT WRITING ASSIGNMENTS TELL US ABOUT COLLEGE WRITING

Writing assignments are revealing classroom artifacts. Instructors' writing assignments say a great deal about their goals and values, as well as the goals and values of their disciplines. Writing assignments are a rich source of information about the rhetorical contexts of writing across the curriculum—a source that few composition researchers have made the focus of significant study. Consider, for example, the following assignment from a European history course at Cornell University:

ESSAY 2: DOCUMENTARY ANALYSIS

This assignment requires you to play the detective, combining textual sources for clues and evidence to form a reconstruction of past events. If you took A.P. history courses in high school, you may recall doing similar document-based questions.

In a tight, well-argued essay of two to four pages, identify and assess the historical significance of the documents in one of the four sets I have given you.

You bring to this assignment a limited body of outside knowledge gained from our readings, class discussions, and videos. Make the most of this contextual knowledge when interpreting your sources.

Questions to consider when planning your essay:

- What do the documents reveal about the author and his audience?
- Why were they written?
- Can you discern the author's motivation and tone?
- Does the genre make a difference in your interpretation?
- How do the documents fit in both their immediate and greater historical contexts?
- Do your documents support or contradict what other sources have told you?
- Is there a contrast between documents within your set?
- What is not said, but implied?
- What is left out? (As a historian, you should always look for what is not said, and ask yourself what the omission signifies.)

Because of the nature of the assignment, you will probably not have an overarching thesis, as you would in most papers. Instead, your essay will consist of two parts: the IDENTIFICATION and INTERPRETATION sections.

Even though this assignment is brief, it defines important rhetorical contexts for writing, such as purpose, audience, and genre. The assignment requires "analysis" and "interpretation," and both thinking strategies are described in ways that are specific to the discourse community of historians. Although the primary audience for the assignment is the teacher, the implied audience can be seen as fellow historians, since students are asked to play the role of discourse community insiders ("As a historian, you should always look for what is not said, and ask yourself what the omission signifies"). The genre of the assignment is also associated with the work of historians, and the instructor reminds students throughout the assignment that a documentary analysis is more than just a template: it's a fundamental part of the work of historians. What is valued in this genre, and in this instructor's notion of the work of historians, is clear from the questions students should consider when planning their essays: quality of analysis, integration of contextual knowledge, and close and careful interpretation.

I would argue that writing assignments like the documentary analysis above are as rich a source of data about college writing as instructor comments or student papers, and *Assignments across the Curriculum* provides a macro-level view of this fundamental classroom artifact. To frame the analysis of the 2,101 writing assignments in the data, I look at the rhetorical situation presented in each assignment (the purposes and audiences), the genres of the assignments, and what these assignments reveal about the discourse communities in which they are situated. The collection of writing assignments tell a complex story of college writing—one that is sometimes disheartening, sometimes encouraging, and hopefully always instructive to composition instructors, writing center tutors, and those involved in WAC initiatives. It's a story about college writing in the United States that provides arguments for both the continued need for campus WAC efforts as well as the positive influence the WAC movement has had on college writing on campuses where WAC has truly taken root.

THE RESEARCH DESIGN

In order to provide a panoramic view of college writing in the United States, *Assignments across the Curriculum* emulates the scope of James Britton and his research team's landmark study (Britton et al. 1975). However, as a single researcher I knew it would be too burdensome to rely on surveying hundreds of instructors or trying to contact instructors individually. The

Internet, and the easy access it offers to instructors' writing assignments, provided the solution. Thanks to the Internet, I was able to gather a collection of artifacts of writing across the curriculum that equaled the sample size of that of Britton's research team. From 1999 to 2007, I collected 2,101 writing assignments from 100 postsecondary institutions across the United States. Because the assignments were collected from the Internet, the research has one important advantage over the surveys of writing across disciplines mentioned earlier. Chris Anson (1988) says of these WAC surveys, "Because most surveys are responded to by choice, even a relatively good return may still represent a skewed sample" (12). As Anson points out, instructors filling out these surveys may exaggerate the importance of writing or the amount of writing in their classes, either to put themselves in a positive light or in an attempt to give the researchers what the instructor thinks they want.

Despite the advantage of the ability to collect a large amount of writing assignments without having to ask for samples from instructors, conducting research via the Internet comes with its own set of problems. Although the assignments I collected were not given voluntarily, the fact that instructors published their assignments on the Internet means they were aware of at least the possibility of a more public audience. Instructors who create their own class websites could be considered "early adopters" of technology, and it's possible that their assignments are fuller or more explicitly laid out than the assignments of instructors who are not using websites. Despite these problems inherent in my study, the advantages of studying a large sample of assignments anonymously outweigh the disadvantages of collecting data from the Internet.

It's important to emphasize that although the assignments in this study were collected from course websites, none of the courses were delivered entirely online. In order to aim for a random and geographically disperse sample, I visited institutional websites through an index of the home pages of accredited colleges in the United States, found at www.utexas.edu/world/univ/. I entered the term "syllabus" in each institution's search engine and used the first course syllabus that appeared in each of the four categories of natural sciences, social sciences, business, and humanities. An even number of institutions were surveyed in four categories based on the Carnegie Classification of Institutions of Higher Education: doctoral/research universities, master's comprehensive colleges, baccalaureate colleges, and two-year A.A. colleges (see appendix A for a list of institutions surveyed). In addition to collecting writing assignments, I gathered other online course materials, such as course descriptions, rubrics, writing guides, etc.

Assignments across the Curriculum meets the bar set by Britton's large-scale research, but one cannot make generalizations about all of college writing in the United States from my sample. According to the National Center for Education Statistics, there were approximately 4,300 US degree-granting postsecondary institutions in 2006–2007, the same time this study was being researched. This means that, with a 95 percent confidence level and 5 percent margin of error, a researcher would need to collect writing assignments from approximately 350 institutions—a difficult task for a team of researchers, much less a single researcher. Although I won't make claims from my sample about all college writing in the United States, I do feel that the prominence of certain patterns in my study can help us make stronger hypotheses about the purposes, audiences, and genres of college writing than we can make with data from a single institution or a handful of institutions. These patterns are discussed through a framework that begins with the rhetorical situations of the assignments—the purposes and audiences—and expands to include the genres of the assignments and the assignments' discourse community contexts.

RHETORICAL SITUATION, GENRE, AND DISCOURSE COMMUNITY: A FRAMEWORK FOR ANALYZING ACADEMIC DISCOURSE

Given the desire to emulate the scope of James Britton et al.'s (1975) study, I naturally used Britton's influential taxonomy of functions and audiences as one tool for analyzing the assignments collected. Britton's taxonomy was appealing in part because I wished to replicate Britton's work, applying his taxonomy to writing assignments rather than student writing, but still focusing like Britton did on purposes and audiences for writing. Britton's function and audience categories—and his divisions of writing functions into transactional, poetic, and expressive—are still used in WAC scholarship and faculty development workshops. For example, Britton's taxonomy is used throughout John Bean's (2011) *Engaging Ideas*, arguably the most popular WAC faculty development guidebook, and his taxonomy is referenced in a collection of essays discussing the future of WAC, *WAC for the New Millennium*. Drawing on Britton's taxonomy of discourse gives my research both a connection to the seminal work of the past and a usefulness in the present. Although this study draws heavily on Britton's taxonomy, the recent scholarship in genre and discourse studies has helped me expand upon Britton's taxonomy and present what I argue is a richer way of thinking about WAC—by moving beyond Britton's sole focus on the rhetorical situation of function and audience. Britton and his team conducted their research prior to the growth of genre and discourse studies, and any current analysis of college literacy should include these added dimensions. Carol Berkenkotter and Thomas Huckin argue, "One way to study the textual character of disciplinary communication is to examine both the situated actions of writers, and the communicative systems in which disciplinary actors participate" (Berkenkotter and Huckin 1994, ix). A framework of rhetorical situation, genre, and discourse community accounts for the "situated action of writers," the repeated and typified actions, and the disciplinary contexts that shape rhetorical situations.

Anne Beaufort's model of academic ways of knowing has been especially useful to me in shaping a framework that moves beyond Britton's taxonomy. Based on her longitudinal study of a student writing in college and the workplace, Beaufort (2007) created a model of five overlapping domains of situated writing knowledge: discourse community knowledge, subject matter knowledge, genre knowledge, rhetorical knowledge, and writing process knowledge. Britton's taxonomy is useful in analyzing the rhetorical knowledge domain of writing assignments, but I also wanted to look at other domains discussed by Beaufort, especially genre and discourse community knowledge, which I saw as helpful additions to Britton's discourse taxonomy. Thus, in addition to the rhetorical situations of this study's writing assignments, I consider groups of assignments that ask students to respond in similar ways to rhetorical situations—"genres." I also consider the social context in which those genres operate—the discourse communities of different academic disciplines. Figure 1.1 provides a visual representation of this expanded framework for thinking about academic discourse. This framework is a tool for analyzing academic

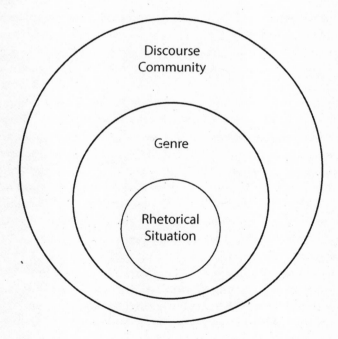

Figure 1.1. A framework for analyzing academic discourse

discourse, but it may also be useful in designing composition courses and WAC workshops, as I discuss in chapter 6. In the rest of this section, I discuss this framework of rhetorical situation, genre, and discourse community.

Rhetorical Situation: The Purposes and Audiences of College Writing

James Britton's multidimensional taxonomy for analyzing written discourse—familiar to many readers of this book—divides writing into three functions, which roughly correspond to different points on the rhetorical triangle: composer (the expressive function), text (the poetic function), and audience (the transactional function). Expressive writing is informal and exploratory, with the self as audience. Poetic writing is imaginative, with a focus on the text as art form. The goal of transactional writing is to transact with an audience, and Britton further divides this function into writing that informs (informative) and writing that persuades (conative).

Based on Timothy Crusius's (1989) critique of Britton's categories, which Crusius feels lack a place for informal writing for an audience beyond the self, this study adds a fourth function to Britton's taxonomy: exploratory. Like expressive assignments, exploratory assignments are informal and focus on exploring ideas, but the audience is public rather than individual. Common examples in this study of exploratory writing are reading responses posted on an electronic bulletin board, which are read and often responded to by peers and the instructor. With the exception of the addition of this "exploratory" function, I utilize Britton's taxonomy to analyze the functions of the writing assignments in my research, but use the more familiar term "purpose" rather than Britton's "function."

This study also borrows from Britton's taxonomy in its analysis of the audiences students are asked to address. I divide audience into four categories: the self, the teacher, peers, and wider audiences. The teacher category is further subdivided into "student to examiner," in which the student provides the "correct" information to the teacher, and "student to instructor," in which the student is not required to merely regurgitate information. Borrowing from Britton, I break the "wider" audience category into an informed, "insider" audience with specialized knowledge on the topic, a novice audience, and a generalized academic reader. Like Britton, I coded for the dominant purpose or audience when more than one was evident (see appendix B for sample coded assignments). Coding the purposes and audiences of assignments is an inexact science (Britton's team of like-minded researchers could only achieve a 63.5 percent inter-rater reliability), but the dominance of certain easily recognizable genres with explicit purposes and audiences—especially short-answer exam writing to inform the teacher as examiner—made the task easier. In chapter 2, I discuss the results of my analysis of the rhetorical situations in various writing assignments.

The Genres of College Writing

As Britton et al. (1975, 1) admits, "there is no satisfactory way of classifying pieces of writing"; although Britton's taxonomy was a useful starting point, it didn't capture the rhetorical features of the assignment, which were broader and more complex than purpose and audience. It also failed to provide a sense of which college writing rhetorical situations were common and "typified," to use Carolyn Miller's (1994) term for describing genres. Aviva Freedman and Peter Medway argue that Britton's taxonomy is limited because it fails to consider the complexities of genre (Freedman and Medway 1994, 12), an understandable omission considering Britton and his team conducted their research prior to the growth of genre studies. Examining purposes, audiences, *and* genres is one way to begin to account for the complexity of the rhetorical features in college writing assignments.

Rather than simply classifying genres by formal features, as surveys of college writing conducted prior to the growth of genre studies had done (Bridgeman and Carlson 1984; Eblen 1983; Harris and Hult 1985), this study follows the lead of recent work in genre studies (Bazerman and Paradis 1991; Devitt 2008; Miller 1994; Swales 1990) and defines genres as responses to recurring rhetorical situations rather than simple templates of form and format. As these theorists argue, genres are impossible to deduce from the structure of the discourse act alone. Rather than imposing static categories on dynamic uses of language by classifying genres by formal features, the aim of this study is to provide a sense of the rhetorical context of writing assignment genres: their purposes and audiences, their social exigencies, and how they vary from discipline to discipline and instructor to instructor. I focus on genre in chapter 2 with an extended look at the two most prominent genres in my study: research papers and exams.

The Discourse Communities of College Writing

Any discussion of academic genres would be incomplete without consideration of the context in which genres occur: the communities of writers and readers who use genre to make meaning. As Beaufort (2012) argues, when genre theory is "used alone as a tool for assignment design and writing instruction, such theory conflates the construct of genres with larger social constructs, such as discourse communities or activity systems" (480). Beaufort suggests that discourse communities "need to be accounted for" in any WAC research (481), and in my research I discuss what writing assignments reveal about the discourse communities of academic disciplines, as well as the broader discourse community of academic writing in the United States, represented by the 100 institutions in the study. My research explores two primary questions regarding academic discourse communities: Is there such a thing as "academic writing"? And in what ways are expectations for writing similar and different across courses in the same discipline? These are the kinds of questions that lend themselves to the macro scale of this study.

To get at a suitable definition of the slippery term "discourse community," I rely on the work of John Swales (1990), who posits the following qualities:

- A discourse community has a broadly agreed set of common public goals.
- A discourse community has mechanisms of intercommunication among its members.
- A discourse community uses its participatory mechanisms primarily to provide information and feedback.
- A discourse community utilizes and hence possesses one or more genres in the communicative furtherance of its aims.
- In addition to owning genres, a discourse community has acquired some specific lexis.
- A discourse community has a threshold level of members with a suitable degree of relevant content and discoursal experience. (24–27)

Using Swales's definition, I ask of the assignments in my research: Is there a broadly shared set of goals across all the assignments, or within specific disciplines? Are there shared academic genres across and/or within disciplines? What discoursal experience is needed to be a successful academic writer?

My hope is that readers will find the framework of rhetorical situation, genre, and discourse community a useful update of Britton et al.'s (1975) taxonomy, one that takes into account the current scholarship in genre and discourse studies, while also largely retaining the taxonomy of his seminal research and replicating it at the college level. As discussed in chapter 6, this updated framework can be used by composition instructors as a way of thinking about curriculum design, by composition studies researchers as a means of analyzing academic discourse, and by WAC practitioners as a faculty development tool.

RESEARCH QUESTIONS

Chris Anson's (1988) questions regarding what it means to write in particular academic disciplines, and how criteria for good writing differ among diverse disciplines, were my foundation as I developed research questions that the data—the collection of 2,101 undergraduate writing assignments from four disciplines—could begin to answer. As I considered the landmark work of Britton, the more recent work of WAC ethnographers, the scholarship in genre and discourse studies, and my own initial reading of the assignments in my collection, I shaped a number of research questions:

- What purposes are students asked to write for in different disciplines?
- What audiences are students asked to address? What role are they asked to play as writers? What role do instructors play as audience?
- What genres are students asked to write in? How do these genres vary from discipline to discipline and instructor to instructor? What is the rhetorical context for these genres?
- How do academic discourse communities differ? Is there a generalized definition of academic discourse that crosses disciplines?
- How do assignments vary across types of institutions, between upper and lower division courses, and between courses associated with a WAC program or initiative and those not connected to WAC?

From reading Britton, I knew that one of the benefits of a large-scale study of writing would be the ability to note significant patterns using a quantitative method. Britton's overwhelming quantitative data about the number of secondary school writing assignments that were merely informative writing to the teacher-as-examiner both depressed and impressed me, and the numbers in my research tell a similar—and similarly overwhelming—story. But numbers only portray part of the story, and the rich textual evidence found in the writing assignment descriptions—and related classroom artifacts such as grading rubrics, writing guides, and course outcomes—provide equally valuable qualitative data. I present both quantitative distribution tables of writing assignment characteristics as well as textual evidence from the assignments.

WRITING TO LEARN AND WRITING IN THE DISCIPLINES: A MULTIPLE-LENS APPROACH TO ANALYZING COLLEGE WRITING

In addition to using quantitative and qualitative data to analyze and report the results of the research, this study uses multiple theoretical lenses to consider the implications of those findings. In order to present a sophisticated interpretation of the findings that takes into account the multiple approaches of the WAC movement, this study considers the purposes, audiences, and genres of the writing assignment through the two primary approaches (or lenses) to WAC: Writing to Learn (WTL) and Writing in the Disciplines (WID). The WTL approach focuses on bringing expressivist pedagogies—such as freewriting and journaling—to instructors across disciplines. Often associated with founding WAC movement theorists and practitioners such as Art Young (1982), Toby Fulwiler (Fulwiler and Young 1982), and James Britton (Britton et al. 1975), the WTL approach encourages teachers across disciplines to see writing as a tool for student learning and self-exploration.

The WID approach—sometimes referred to as "learning to write" or "learning to write in the disciplines"—is also focused on shifting more attention to writing across the curriculum, but emphasizes the investigation of writing in different academic discourse communities to help instructors initiate students into those discourse communities of their disciplines. WID theorists, such as Anne Herrington (1985) and Charles Bazerman (Bazerman and Paradis 1991) tend to focus on WAC as a means of helping students prepare for academic discourse. Part of this preparation includes understanding the sociopolitical contexts of initiation into academic disciplines.

Whether it was James Britton's (Britton et al. 1975) discouragement over the absence of expressive writing required of British secondary school students, or Mike Rose's (1983) creation of a first-year writing curriculum based on disciplinary writing expectations from his survey of UCLA faculty writing assignments, a number of prior researchers who investigated WAC on a large scale predominately used either a WTL or WID lens to consider the significance and implications of their research. Researchers looking at their data through a WTL lens tended to focus on what was missing from academic discourse, rather than fully considering the richness of the disciplinary knowledge reflected in their data. Conversely, researchers looking at their data through a WID lens often fail to see some of the ways that academic writing might limit student expression or their ability to make personal connections to the subjects they are studying and writing about.

Prominent WAC theorists have claimed that this WTL/ WID split in WAC research and practice is artificial, and they argue for a dialogue between the two approaches (Jones and Comprone 1993; McLeod and Maimon 2000; McLeod and Miraglia 2001; Thaiss 2001). McLeod and Miraglia (2001) discuss this need for integration in their chapter "Writing Across the Curriculum in a Time of Change" in the book *WAC for the Millennium*:

> We cannot emphasize too strongly that it is an error to see writing to learn and writing to communicate as somehow in conflict with each other. Most of us who have been involved in WAC programs from the beginning see "writing to learn" and "writing to communicate" as two complementary, even synergistic, approaches to writing across the curriculum, approaches that can be integrated in individual classrooms as well as in entire programs. (5)

I agree with McLeod and Miraglia, that neither a WTL or WID approach alone is an adequate way of thinking about how composition instructors and WAC practitioners might approach the writing that happens across disciplines. Rather than viewing the results through a single, "terministic screen," to use Kenneth Burke's (1969) phrase, this study considers the assignments from both WTL and WID perspectives. This multiple-lens approach is especially valuable because the findings of the study suggest the influence of both approaches, as well as points of connection between them. For example, the research reveals a dominance of short-answer exam writing that both WTL and WID approaches can effectively address, and it indicates that both approaches to faculty development have had a powerful and positive influence on instructors who are teaching in courses explicitly linked with a WAC initiative, with the two approaches often working together in an instructor's sequence of assignments. At the end of each chapter, and especially in chapter 6, I consider the implications of my findings through both WTL and WID lenses, and I work to connect the two approaches.

In the following chapters, then, I provide a framework for thinking about academic discourse that expands on the work of Britton and integrates current scholarship in genre and discourse studies, as well a way to interpret findings from studies of WAC that takes into account and integrates the multiple lenses of WTL and WID.

OUTLINE OF THE BOOK

In chapter 2, I discuss the rhetorical situations—the purposes and audiences—of the 2,101 writing assignments in the study. This chapter provides both a statistical breakdown of the purposes and audiences students are asked to write to in the assignments and a close textual analysis of these purposes and audiences. Included in chapter 2 are examples from assignment descriptions as well as related materials often available on the class websites, such as syllabi, rubrics, course learning outcomes, writing guides, etc. This chapter relies on Britton et al.'s (1975) taxonomy of function (purpose) and audience, while adding "exploratory" purposes for writing, defined as informal writing to a wider audience, such as electronic discussion board journal posts. My research, like Britton's, reveals limited purposes and audiences for writing, with informative writing to the teacher-as-examiner predominant across disciplines and at every level, from first-year introductory courses to senior seminars.

Chapter 3 moves from the individual rhetorical situations of the writing assignments to repeated, "typified" rhetorical situations with similar purposes, audiences, forms, and formats— "genres." In light of recent work in genre studies, chapter 3 considers not the formal features of genres, but their social action—their rhetorical contexts and how they might shape students' experiences of various disciplines. To this end, rather than simply doing a head count of genres, I look closely at the rhetorical contexts of the two predominant genres in the study:

research papers and short-answer exams. I argue that the kinds of extended research writing found in the study might cause both compositionists and WAC theorists to rethink stereotypes of the research writing our students are assigned outside of composition classes. Unfortunately, the predominance of short-answer exams in the genre data confirms some of our worst fears about the limited ways instructors use writing outside of composition classes. This may cause WAC theorists to rethink current beliefs about the varieties of genres students encounter as they enter into and progress through their majors.

Chapter 4 discusses writing assignments in the broader context of discourse communities, exploring the question, "Are there qualities of academic writing that academic discourse communities have in common?" Chapter 4 discusses the ways these assignments reveal differences across academic discourse communities, including significant differences in what instructors within the same sub-disciplines value in student writing. This chapter presents a paradox that speaks to the complexity of academic discourse as represented in the assignments: there is a generic notion of academic discourse that cuts across disciplines, while at the same time there are significant enough differences between disciplines and among teachers in the same discipline that the term "discourse community" is slippery at best.

Of the 400 courses in the research, 12 were affiliated in some way with a WAC initiative. These were courses labeled "writing intensive," courses offered by instructors in a multidisciplinary campus writing unit or connected to an adjunct peer tutoring program. Chapter 5 looks more closely at these WAC courses in order to support an argument for the important influence WAC has had on writing education. Chapter 5 illustrates that the writing assignments from courses connected to a WAC initiative truly stand out as richer and more complex. The WAC courses provide students with more sophisticated and more clearly articulated rhetorical contexts, a greater variety of genres, more opportunities for revision and feedback, and more writing overall than those not connected to a WAC initiative.

Although I build on chapter 5 to make an argument for the value of WAC in my conclusions in chapter 6, I also argue that the dominance of informing to the teacher-as-examiner, and the genre of the short-answer exam, point to the continued and pressing need of the WAC movement as a tool for reform. Because I view my results through the multiple lenses of WTL and WID, I argue for the significance of my findings on multiple fronts: WTL researchers would be pleased with the amount of exploratory journal writing I discovered, but would bemoan the continued absence of expressive writing. WID researchers would be especially interested in the kinds of extended research writing I found, and what the writing assignments reveal about academic discourse communities. Both WTL and WID researchers would see some of the limits of the assignments in the study—especially the predominance of short-answer exam writing—and the positive influence of WAC initiatives on writing assignments as arguments for the continued need for and value of WAC efforts. In this final chapter, I discuss the implications of my findings for first-year writing instructors, writing center tutors, and WAC workshop leaders.

2

LIMITED PURPOSES, NARROW AUDIENCES
The Rhetorical Situations of College Writing

Stephen Wilhoit argues, "at the heart of every assignment is the rhetorical situation—someone writing to someone about something for some purpose" (Wilhoit 2002, 62). From Lloyd Bitzer to Wayne Booth to James Britton, compositionists have focused on the composer and the audience as fundamental components of rhetorical acts. Although I also consider the broader contexts of genre and discourse community in my framework for analyzing the 2,101 writing assignments from across the curriculum in my research, the starting point for my analysis and the focus of the present chapter involves the rhetorical situation of purpose and audience.

This chapter presents the results of an analysis of the purposes and audiences of writing assignments from across the curriculum in 400 different courses at 100 postsecondary institutions. Although I cannot generalize all college writing in the United States from my sample, I believe this chapter reveals a convincing—and often disappointing—pattern that speaks to the limited purposes and audiences instructors in my research assign.

This chapter includes both the quantitative distributions of purpose and audience, and a textual analysis of representative assignments and related materials available on class websites, such as grading rubrics and course outcomes. Despite the limited rhetorical situations students are asked to address in college writing, the textual analysis reveals that the courses that

DOI: 10.7330/9780874219401.c002

demand of students some of the richest and most varied rhetorical situations are those courses connected in some way to a WAC
initiative—a finding discussed more fully in chapter 5.

THE PURPOSES OF COLLEGE WRITING

In both Britton et al.'s (1975) large-scale study of British secondary school writing and Applebee, Lehr, and Auten's (1981)
large-scale study of American secondary school writing, the
researchers found that writing for a transactional purpose, especially writing to inform, dominated the assignments they collected. Sixty-three percent of the 2,122 pieces of student writing
in Britton's collection had a transactional purpose, with informative function accounting for 62 percent of transactional writing. Just 17 percent of assignments had a poetic purpose, and
only 5 percent were expressive. Transactional writing was even
more predominant in Applebee's research. Surveys of college
courses by Bridgeman and Carlson (1984) and Eblen (1983)
reveal similar results: writing to transact—in particular, writing
to inform—was the dominant purpose.

My research shows results similar to prior studies, as Table 2.1
outlines. Of the 2,101 assignments collected, writing for a transactional purpose accounts for 83 percent, and most transactional
assignments (66 percent) are informative rather than persuasive.
Although a significant amount of writing is for an exploratory
purpose (13 percent), poetic and expressive writing are almost
non-existent. These distributions are across similar types of institutions and at both lower and upper divisions. I'd originally
planned to investigate the differences in writing purposes among
disciplines, among introductory and upper-level courses, and
among different types of institutions, but I quickly realized that
there are no significant differences. Sixty-four percent of upper-
division writing was informative, with only 3 percent of writing
expressive and 0.4 percent poetic. In contrast to Sommers and
Saltz's (2004) findings regarding Harvard instructors' emphasis
on writing as constructing new knowledge through research, at
the "elite" colleges in my study (institutions such as UC Berkeley,

Duke, and Cornell), 69 percent of writing was to inform, and only 1 percent of writing had expressive or poetic purposes. At every type of institution and at each level—from community colleges to "elite" institutions, from introductory courses to senior seminars—writing to inform was the dominant purpose.

Table 2.1. Distribution of the purposes of writing

Purpose	Number of Assignments	Percentage of Total
Transactional (total)	1,751	83
Informative	1,399	66
Persuasive	352	17
Expressive	62	3
Exploratory	279	13
Poetic	9	Less than 1%

Most of the assignments with an informative purpose give students an extremely limited view of academic discourse, instead asking them to simply display the "right" answer or the "correct" definition to the instructor through a recall of facts—what Applebee calls "writing without composing" (Applebee, Lehr, and Auten 1981, 18). Typically the required information comes from lecture material or the textbook, rather than the students' own experiences, as these exam questions illustrate:

In your textbook, Steven Smith describes three different roles legislators might play in representing their constituents. List and describe each of these three.

Describe the major factors causing changes in food consumption (see Chpts. 1–4) and describe the marketing channel for a chosen commodity (see Chpt. 12).

Explain the principles of government identified in the text and in class as characterizing our system under the constitution.

From my outline on earthquakes, explain the "effects" of earthquakes.

Short-answer and essay exams make up 21 percent of the assignments, and the majority of informative writing is "student to examiner." Only 17 percent of transactional writing asks students for persuasive writing for an audience other than the teacher-as-examiner. Sometimes this examiner role is further emphasized in the assignment criteria. For example, according to an exam question, an environmental science instructor is looking for "phrases and sentences that show me what you know about a topic." An international business instructor went so far as to tell students that "the answers should be composed to inform the reader. In the end, I am the reader, so you are writing to inform me." This kind of emphasis on providing the correct answer to the teacher-as-examiner isn't limited to short-answer exams. The "informal" response journals in a British literature course, for example, represent an extreme case of writing to inform as writing to provide a correct answer. In the assignment description for a journal that asked students to interpret an ode from Wordsworth, the instructor writes:

> I see only one way to interpret these stanzas. You may interpret some of the details in a slightly different way, but there is a well-established way to interpret the stanzas that makes perfect sense, that explains all of the details of the lines, and that is consistent with the ideas explained in the introduction to the poem and conveyed elsewhere in the poem. Yes, I'm looking for a specific and correct answer here!

A sociology instructor puts in his syllabus an explanation of essay response marks, including the symbol "?" for "Do you really think so. I doubt it"; "??" for "Are you serious?"; "x" for "This is not correct"; and "No" for "You have badly misinterpreted the reading. I'm unhappy." A majority of the assignments in my study reinforce David Bartholomae's (1986) argument in his classic article on academic discourse, "Inventing the University":

> Much of the written work students do is test-taking, report or summary, work that places them outside the working discourse of the academic community, where they are expected to admire and report on what we do, rather than inside that discourse, where they can do its work and participate in a common enterprise. (144)

Assignments that have a persuasive purpose often begin with the kind of summary or explanation found in informative writing, but persuasive assignments require students to go one step further and argue a position, moving students closer to Bartholomae's notion of working inside the discourse rather than outside it. These instructions for a review of an environmental article from a writing-intensive course illustrate this point: "Do give a brief summary of the paper in your review, but DON'T stop there. You should also undertake some analysis—DO some original thinking of your own!" A social science instructor uses similar language in her instructions for an essay on welfare policy: "The purpose of this paper is to stimulate your thinking about 'social or distributive justice.' You are to develop your own position on this topic. Specifically, what principles should guide government in determining what to guarantee its citizens?" One philosophy instructor uses Bloom's (1956) taxonomy to contrast informative and persuasive writing: "The point of the essay is not merely to answer the questions, but primarily to justify your answers, using reasons drawn from the texts and from reflections on these theories. For fans of Bloom's taxonomy, the essays begin at the knowledge and comprehension levels and move beyond comprehension to application."

Since the persuasive purpose is aligned with the "audience" component of the rhetorical triangle, it's not surprising that many of the assignments with a persuasive purpose provide students with a hypothetical audience beyond the instructor. In the assignment description for an application letter, a management communication instructor writes: "Note that your application letter is an 'argument'; that is, it tries to persuade the reader to act in alignment with your aims. A proposal is written to persuade an audience to act favorably on a solution to a documented problem." This connection to an audience is seen again in an essay for an international business course, in which students must "recommend an action based on argumentative claims" and "provide a rationale for your recommendations to the management team at a company." As I discuss in detail in chapter 5, instructors in courses connected to a WAC initiative assigned significantly more persuasive writing and significantly less informative writing.

Expressive and poetic writing were even rarer than persuasive writing. Just sixty-two of the assignments called on students to produce expressive writing, with the majority of these assignments coming from courses connected to a WAC initiative. These assignments are mostly "free-writes," written to an audience of the self and with the goal of invention. One caveat I need to note is that since I didn't observe classes or interview instructors, I didn't capture in-class writing, which is more likely to have an expressive purpose. Expressive writing is also most often ungraded, so it is not likely to be noted on course descriptions and syllabi. However, given the dominance of the traditional lecture/exam found in the syllabi and assignments I collected, I'm skeptical that a significant amount of instructors in my research—other than those connected to a WAC initiative—are using expressive in-class writing.

Britton found that each year students progressed through the British public school system they did less and less writing for expressive and poetic purposes. Perhaps this is doubly true as students move from high school to college in America, speculating from my collection of assignments. Although Britton found that 17 percent of the writing in his research was poetic, my research includes only nine assignments whose dominant aim was poetic. These assignments include a play monologue in an introduction to theater course, an imaginative description of a natural setting in a nature literature course, and a retelling of an ancient myth in a Western humanities course.

The dominance of informative writing and the absence of expressive and poetic writing in my research are similar to the results of previous studies. Where my findings differ from prior research is in the number of journaling assignments, which typically asked students to explore ideas, often for an audience that included peers. Previous surveys of college writing (Eblen 1983; Rose 1983) found that exploratory writing—and the genre of the journal—was rare. In a popular WAC faculty development guide, *Engaging Ideas,* John Bean argues that students are not given nearly enough opportunities for exploratory writing (Bean 2011, 121). In my research, however, exploratory journals and their computer age equivalent, the electronic discussion board, are a common phenomenon, seeming to indicate rapid growth in exploratory journal writing in the last thirty years. Although assignments that call on students to use technology like blogs, hypertext, wikis, etc. were rare in my research, the use of electronic discussion boards for exploratory writing was frequent. Given the time frame in which I conducted my research, it's likely that instructors are now making more use of technologies like blogs, wikis, and electronic discussion boards, resulting in even more exploratory writing.

The instructors in my research see exploratory writing as a way to encourage students to invent arguments, make connections, reflect on personal experience, and take risks. The following descriptions for journal assignments illustrate this use of exploratory writing:

> The journal is a space for you to investigate your own thoughts, reactions, and feelings on particular art ideas and art works. I'm asking you to make connections between what you are learning and what you have already experienced.

> Logs are designed to keep you up to date with the readings, to stimulate class discussion, and to encourage you to think about the class materials as both psychological scholarship and as personally relevant.

> Treat the e-mail messages as an opportunity to express freely your own thoughts, opinions, observations, and questions. You may also use them to float preliminary ideas for your essays. Because they are informal you needn't be overly concerned with structure, organization, and rhetorical polish.

> Think of it as a conversation in writing, or as pre-talking analogous to the pre-writing you do for papers. Our goal is not to produce expertly crafted individual treatises, but to develop the ability to think, respond, and communicate through writing. Your contributions should be informal, spontaneous, informed, and impassioned.

I found that exploratory writing was assigned across disciplines. The previous passages are from courses in art history, psychology, environmental studies, and poetry, respectively. Although there are no personal diary journals in my study, journals were more or less the only genre in my research that allowed students to test ideas and take risks, to use personal experience, and to respond to peers.

As the passages above reveal, instructors are using journals for both WTL and WID purposes. Journals are one example of how WTL and WID purposes can be integrated in an assignment. When the instructors ask students to use journal writing to "think about the class materials as both psychological scholarship and as personally relevant," or to "express freely your own thoughts" and "float preliminary ideas for your essays," there is really no distinction between writing as personal and writing as disciplinary initiation. As further discussed in chapter 5, journal writing assignments are especially popular among the courses in my collection that are in some way connected to a WAC initiative, perhaps as a writing intensive or WID requirement. The popularity of journal writing in this study may speak to the influence of the WAC movement.

THE AUDIENCES FOR COLLEGE WRITING

Both Britton and Applebee found that most of the secondary school student writing they collected was written for the teacher, and most commonly the teacher-as-examiner. Of Britton et al.'s (1975) samples, 86 percent were written for the teacher, and in 48 percent of those the teacher played the role of examiner. In Applebee, Lehr, and Auten's (1981) study, 55 percent of school writing was directed to the teacher-as-examiner. As Table 2.2 indicates, the audience distributions in my study are similar to Britton's and Applebee's. In 64 percent of the student writing assignments, the teacher-as-examiner is the audience. Just as I was curious if upper-division courses in my research require less informative writing than lower-division courses, I wondered if students wrote for audiences beyond the teacher—especially the teacher-as-examiner—as they moved from introductory courses to upper-division courses in their major. I speculated that the junior- and senior-level courses in my study would require students to write in disciplinary genres aimed at a wider readership than just the instructor: for example, readers of disciplinary journals or grant committees. However, just as informative writing dominated all levels of instruction in my research, the prevailing audience for these assignments was "student to examiner." In upper-division courses, 61 percent of writing had the audience of teacher-as-examiner. The prevalence of the examiner audience holds across types of institutions as well. The instructor plays the examiner role in 64 percent of writing in the "elite" colleges in my research.

Table 2.2. Distribution of the audiences for writing

Audience	Number of Assignments	Percentage of Total
Student to Examiner	1343	64
Student to Instructor (general)	388	18
Peers	117	6
Self	111	5
Wider Audience (total)	142	7
Informed	89	4
Novice	29	2
Generalized Reader	24	1

Coding assignments "student to examiner" wasn't difficult: nearly two out of every three assignments was directed to the audience of the teacher-as-examiner, and nearly one out of every four assignments was a short-answer exam. There were plenty of non-exam assignments that still focused on giving the teacher the right information in the correct format. A psychology teacher who says in his article review assignment, "Show me you understand the subject matter," could be speaking for many of the instructors in my research. And correctness of subject matter wasn't the only way that instructors played the examiner role in my study. In their assignment descriptions and grading rubrics, it was common for instructors to obsess over correct formatting, whether that meant citation style, font, or margins. Take, for example, the British history teacher who warned his students: "I do own a pica measure and a ruler; don't make me use them on your paper."

Some instructors in my research played the role of examiner even when they were responding to rough drafts. A Chinese economy instructor collects a "first draft" that students may revise, but stated: "This is not a rough draft, and will be graded. There should be nothing rough in the mechanics of this paper. This draft should be your best effort at a complete, coherent paper." An anthropology instructor tells students: "Your first draft will be edited, graded, and returned to you." This first draft was worth fifty points, and the final draft was worth one hundred. It seems that students aren't pleased by instructors who collect "rough" drafts and then grade them for mechanics, as this statement from a biology instructor indicates: "Please don't flip out about your grades on the first draft. I graded hard because there is much work to be done on most of the papers and the scores should reflect that. But please don't show up at my apartment with a gun!"

Considering the results of prior WAC surveys of college writing, it's not surprising that 64 percent of the assignments I collected were written to the teacher-as-examiner. A more dramatic statistic, however, is the fact that nearly one out of every three assignments was directed to an *explicitly stated* audience of the teacher-as-examiner. The 29 percent of assignments in this category roughly coincides with the percentage of assignments that are short-answer and essay exams. Perhaps if this prevalence of the stated audience of teacher-as-examiner were only true of the introductory courses in the study, it would be less surprising. After all, introductory courses typically have high enrollment caps. When you have an extremely large class, testing for a correct answer is much easier on the instructor than responding to essay assignments. It was surprising, though, that one-third of all assignments were to a stated audience of teacher-as-examiner, even in senior seminars.

Assignments placed in the "student to instructor (general)" category evidenced a dialogue between instructor and student. Assignments in this category are often done in stages, with the instructor collecting and commenting on a draft of the essay. These instructors establish a dialogue with the student that places them in a "coaching" rather than an "examining" role, as in the case of this political science assignment: "For the term paper listed in your syllabus, you will first submit a draft to me. I will review your essay and suggest ways to improve the argument and style. These comments will raise questions, suggest changes, and provide you with a valuable resource for revising your material for the final draft."

Robert Jones and Joseph Comprone argue, "Teaching process in a single class—freshman comp—cannot ultimately be successful unless the writing in that course is reinforced by the same kind of approach to learning in other courses" (Jones and Comprone 1993, 59). Anecdotal evidence from WAC workshop leaders suggests that, prior to exposure to WAC pedagogy, few instructors in disciplines outside of composition engage students in a writing process. In my research, 50 out of 400 instructors collected at least one rough draft from students. In their assignment descriptions, these instructors usually gave students an encouraging message about process, such as one political science instructor gave in a political philosophy essay assignment: "You will turn in a first version of the essay. This initial essay will be read and critiqued but will be ungraded. I would be more than happy to read a draft of your essay at any time prior to the class period it is due and give you feedback." These instructors respond to drafts and hold one-on-one conferences and peer response workshops because they feel, to quote two writing-intensive business course syllabi, that "writing involves frequent drafting and revising" and "no one writes the final version of anything on the first draft." The surprising amount of multi-draft writing in my research may once again point to the influence of the WAC movement on the instructors of my study. Additionally, as I will discuss in chapter 5, courses connected to a WAC initiative were far more likely to require feedback from peers and/or the instructor during the writing process.

Many of the "student to instructor (general)" assignments were ungraded. A few of the instructors asked students to do a brief "free-write" the first week of class, with students discussing their goals and hopes for the course. For example, one computer programming instructor asked students to write him a letter, in order to help him get a sense of his students as learners: "Tell me of your strengths, weaknesses, goals, and fears. Discuss your worlds and how your roles in those worlds might affect your performance in class." The goal of this assignment, according to the explanation in the assignment prompt, was to help the instructor modify the course to meet the students' needs. It's important to stress, however, that assignments like these are rare in my collection.

In both Britton's and Applebee's research, writing to peers was negligible. Considering the results of previous studies, the fact that 6 percent of the assignments I collected contain the stated or implied audience of peers is significant. It's not surprising that courses that use what Paulo Freire (1970) disparagingly refers to as the "banking method," where instructors "deposit" information to students through lectures and then test them for that information on exams, rarely required writing to peer audiences. It seems that instructors who assign writing to a peer audience do so in order to remove the emphasis on teacher-as-examiner. In an American history course, for example, students wrote a series of research essays that had to be "credible to both peers and instructors." The culmination of the essays included an in-class presentation, where students explained the results of their research to peers. The second research project was written collaboratively, a technique emphasized in the course description: "This class is designed to maximize collaboration between students." Another example comes from a biology course, where the instructor's course description explicitly stated, "The audience (or pretend audience) for all of your written work is your classmates, not the instructor." The instructor used peer response workshops to further emphasize this point. A number of instructors use electronic bulletin board journals as a space for writing to peers, and this emphasis is reinforced by assignments that describe these journals, as one British literature instructor said, as "a conversation in writing."

My research includes three general types of assignments written for the audience of "self": free-writes, a self-assessment written at the beginning or end of the course, and assignments that required students to relate the content of the course to their own lives. One example of a self-assessment assignment comes from an "assessment of learning reflection memo" for a writing-intensive business course. In this memo, students wrote an ungraded self-assessment reflecting on how the course has improved their professional development. An environmental studies course description provides another example: "This is your education, you must be an active participant in it, and it is only you who can determine its value to you, through self-evaluation and reflection."

An example of the third type of writing for the self, relating course content to personal interests and experiences, comes from an anthropology course. Students compared their diet to that of a caveman, partly to "analyze the nutritional quality of the diet of a hunter gatherer," partly to "analyze the nutritional quality of your own diet," and partly to "give you a broader perspective on the relative quality of your own diet." Furthermore, a course in professional selling techniques asked students to keep a "time summary" of how they spent their days "in order to discover what you are doing with those 1440 minutes you have every day." They kept this log because "a salesperson's time is a valuable commodity."

These self-assessments and self-reflection assignments are the kinds of writing that WTL scholars feel can "personalize knowledge" and "represent our experience to our own understanding" (Fulwiler and Young 1982, x, 4). In their meta-analysis of writing-to-learn studies, Bangert-Drowns, Hurley, and Wilkinson (2004) found that these kinds of metacognitive prompts where students could "reflect on their current knowledge, confusions, and learning processes proved particularly effective" (50). In their study of student writers at George Mason University, Chris Thaiss and Terry Myers Zawacki noted that important factors in students' gaining confidence and ability to write proficiently in their majors included

> opportunities for reflecting on their writing; reflecting on the
> rhetorical choices they've made based on purpose, content, and
> audience; on the connections they've discerned among topics,
> formats, and styles; and on their discovery that writing can be
> a means of realizing their own interests and desires as write.
> (Thaiss and Zawacki 2006, 121)

Unfortunately, students in my study are not often called upon to relate course content to personal experiences and interests, use personal experiences to develop and support their arguments, or reflect on their own learning.

In sharp contrast to assignments written to the teacher-as-examiner, assignments written to a wider audience almost always provided students with a real-world rhetorical situation and genre. This is especially true of assignments in the "wider audience: informed" category. Some of the audiences students wrote for in this category included company CEOs, Democratic Party organizers, and readers of the *New England Journal of Medicine*. Usually, these rhetorical situations mirror the kinds of writing students will encounter in the workplace. For example, a management course assignment asked students to "provide group recommendations as if you were a consulting team offering suggestions on how to improve management practices," and a finance course assignment instructed students to "assume that you are just hired as a CFO for a major corporation. The CEO would like you to review some of the major financial decisions for the company."

Sometimes the wider audience was real instead of hypothetical. In a professional selling techniques course, students wrote a business letter to the person who helped them research their essay topics. The instructor collected these letters and mailed them. In a number of other business courses, students wrote application letters and resumes for jobs they were currently applying for. A communications course assignment asked students to create informative websites about a communications topic "that could be used by others as a starting point for researching that topic." In this case, the "general" audience is abstract, yet also very real: students include hit counters so they can see how many people make up their audience. Unlike a short-answer essay exam, students often take on an additonal role, or at least a role different from "novice" student. In a biology course, for example, students play the role of an editor of *The Sciences* journal and respond to a recently published article. In an agricultural marketing course, students play the role of new employees at ACME, and they have to write a report to the boss. In an international economy course, students act as pharmaceutical company employees and write a feasibility report to the company's board of directors. In various other assignments, students play the role of marketing research team members, human resource managers, and business consultants.

Another pattern concerning assignments written to a wider, informed audience is worth noting. The majority of assignments written to audiences such as company CEOs or readers of academic journals introduce students to disciplinary and professional writing by requiring them to write in specific disciplinary genres. Many of the assignments in the "wider audience: informed" category are professional genres: resumes, application letters, memos, and feasibility reports. Instructors who only assign writing to the teacher—and especially writing to inform the teacher-as-examiner—neglect to provide students with the kind of meaningful rhetorical purposes and social contexts found in assignments aimed at wider audiences, and often neglect to give students practice in the academic and professional genres of their disciplines. As Mary Soliday argues, "research consistently suggests students engage more with assignments where they approximate expert roles and grapple with the fields 'true questions'" (2011, 68).

MIXED SIGNALS ABOUT PURPOSE AND AUDIENCE

The dominance of writing to inform to the teacher-as-examiner caused me to sympathize with the students who were taking the courses I studied. These students were all too often asked to use writing to simply parrot information in a limited and monotonous rhetorical situation. I was just as sympathetic to the mixed signals students received from writing assignments regarding purposes and audiences for writing.

One common issue I found is that many of the instructors who claim to value persuasive and exploratory purposes for writing in the learning outcomes on their course syllabi required only lower-level informative tasks like listing, identifying, and explaining in their actual assignments and exam questions. One example of mixed signals comes from a zoology instructor, who, in a section of her website titled "Testing Philosophy," discussed "concrete (first-order thinking) vs. formal (second-order) thinking":

> Although many high schools are now placing emphasis on critical analysis, high school biology tests have traditionally consisted of simply regurgitating facts onto an exam. At the college level, you should be able to take the facts and apply them to a new situation. This application is called second-order thinking or formal thinking. Here is an example of a first-order question: What kind of animal has a long intestine compared to its body size? Here is an example of a second-order question: Of the following animals, which will have the longest intestine for its body size and why?

Despite the fact that this instructor emphasized second-order thinking, and told her students, "I would expect you to be able to answer questions similar to those posed through the analysis level [of Bloom's (1956) taxonomy]," the actual exams required mostly first-order thinking. The exams were dominated by multiple choice and fill-in-the-blank questions, with a few essay questions where students were required to explain evolutionary processes or functions. In the "Testing Philosophy" section of her course description, this instructor had advice concerning "Basic Errors You Should Never Make":

> If you mix up words that are spelled or sound similar, you will have your answer counted wrong. For example, stating that an ectoderm is an animal that has no insulation to hold in body heat is wrong, wrong, wrong. Do not come to me after an exam and argue about these kinds of mistakes . . . I expect you to learn how to be precise.

A physical science instructor gave students the same kind of mixed signals in her exams. According to her grading rubric, the criteria for an "A" exam included "sophisticated information . . . unusual insights, original thoughts, and flashes of brilliance." The exam questions, however, asked students to recall information from lectures and the textbook. Students must "define latitude and parallel," "list the contributing factors that give rise to the seasons," and "explain the role of cloud cover." These questions left little opportunity for "unusual insights" or "original thoughts." Ironically, the rubric itself was adapted from an article by Barbara Tewksbury titled "Teaching without Exams."

One example of the confusion of "exploring" and "informing" comes from an essay exam in a sociological theories course. Just like the zoology example, this sociology instructor emphasized creativity in the evaluation criteria of her syllabus and implied that her essay exams had an exploratory purpose: "The word 'essay' means 'a try,' as in an attempt to understand. The best essays present an idea in a unique, creative and interesting way." The actual essay questions, however, contradicted the purpose for writing presented in the assignment description. One essay asked students to identify the characteristics of Comte's and Spencer's theories, a second asked students to explain Durkheim's argument about suicide, and a third required students to "briefly outline the concepts of mechanical and organic solidarity according to Durkheim." The keywords here—"identify," "explain," and "outline"—are verbs associated with informative purposes for writing, not exploratory.

In her ethnographic study of two chemical engineering courses, Anne Herrington (1985) found that students were often given mixed signals about audience. For example, the instructor would encourage students to write to a wider audience, but then play the role of examiner when responding to the essay. Similar mixed signals were given to students in the assignments in my research. In a selling techniques course, for example, students videotaped a practice business presentation and then wrote a self-evaluation of the tape. The primary audience for the assignment is the "self," and the teacher encouraged students to discuss how they could improve the presentation. But the teacher also played an examiner role. Despite the fact that the main goal of the assignment was a discussion and evaluation of "self," the teacher wrote: "grammatical errors and misspelled words will result in a significant reduction in your grade—one point for each error." An international business instructor gave students mixed signals in his essay exams when he told students that each essay question would include a rhetorical situation. For example, one question asked the students to act as international business consultants writing to a CEO. In the same assignment description, however, the instructor wrote: "The answers should be composed to inform the reader. In the end, I am the reader, so you are writing to inform me."

Reflection on Purposes and Audiences for College Writing

Toby Fulwiler (Fulwiler and Young 1982) argues that the universe of discourse includes a much broader range of writing purposes and audiences than is normally recognized by teachers, and this is certainly true of the teachers my collection of assignments. I was especially surprised to find that it mattered little if the course was a lower-division survey or a senior seminar—writing to inform the teacher-as-examiner dominated college writing. My research supports Michael Pemberton's (1995) claim that

> the locus of much undergraduate . . . teaching remains rooted in the Freirian "banking model." Instructors and textbooks are regarded as repositories of content information which is disseminated to students, and the students are expected to absorb this information, and, on command, to replay—some would say regurgitate—it. (121)

Britton and Applebee, who were both interested in the value of writing as a tool for thinking and discovery, were disappointed to find that informative writing to the teacher-as-examiner was so prevalent in their samples of British and American secondary school writing. Echoing Britton and Applebee, Fulwiler says that WAC must work "against the dominant view of language in schools: that the function of language is to inform" (Fulwiler and Young 1982, 3). Fulwiler feels that language for learning is different from language for informing. I feel these theorists would see the dominance of informative writing in my sample as an argument for the need for WAC leaders to convince instructors in the disciplines that assigning strictly informative writing "neglects the discovery function of language" (Fulwiler and Young 1982, 6).

Beginning with Janet Emig's (1971) *The Composing Processes of Twelfth Graders*, researchers who have investigated students writing habits both in and out of school have found that, in their self-sponsored writing, students are more likely to write for expressive and poetic purposes. In case studies of twenty high school students, Applebee (1984) found that 39 percent wrote imaginatively when writing for themselves. Art Young (1982) argues, "the creative impulse is central to the development, understanding, and application of knowledge" (78). Young sees creative writing as a valuable way for students to make connections with disciplinary content. Young might argue that the students in my study who write a monologue in an introduction to theater course or an ancient myth in a Western humanities course gain a new appreciation of those genres.

Writing for expressive purposes and making personal connections are also valuable uses that are neglected by the instructors in my research. In their meta-analysis of WTL studies, Bangert-Drowns, Hurley, and Wilkinson (2004) found that expressive writing was particularly effective, supporting the arguments made for decades by WTL theorists such as Britton et al. (1975), Young (1982), and Fulwiler (Fulwiler and Young 1982). In her longitudinal study of students writing across the curriculum at the City University of New York, Marilyn Sternglass (1997) notes that using personal experiences motivates students, and that "integrating material from personal knowledge or experience" is a primary way students construct new knowledge for themselves (22). Similarly, Herrington and Curtis (2000) and Sommers and Saltz (2004) found that, for the students in their longitudinal studies, writing development accelerated when students were allowed to pursue personal interests.

Another reason personal writing is valuable has to do with the politics of initiation to academic discourses. As Donna LeCourt argues, "Making a space for the personal . . . counteracts the students' perceptions that their alternative voices must be silenced within a disciplinary discourse" (1996, 81). The lack of expressive and poetic writing in my research, then, is evidence of the limited uses instructors across disciplines make of writing, and also the limited agency students have to make academic languages their own, or to resist conformity to academic discourses. My findings speak to the continued need for WAC practitioners to help instructors in the disciplines become more aware of the value and uses of writing for expressive and poetic purposes.

The reformist zeal of the early WAC movement has been critiqued for its "missionary" approach, and I agree with Mark Waldo's (2003) belief that WAC workshop leaders need to be aware of the fact that WTL pedagogies such as expressive and poetic writing are not as valued in the disciplines as they are in composition courses. At the same time, WAC practitioners interested primarily in a WID approach to faculty development would also be troubled by my findings. Informative writing to the teacher-as-examiner in the genre of a short-answer exam does little to truly initiate students to the primary purposes and audiences of the writing in their disciplines. The significant differences between the exam assignments and the assignments that asked for persuasive writing to wider audiences in authentic disciplinary genres illustrate the potential learning that is lost when instructors focus on the lecture/exam approach. My research points to a pressing need for WAC to refrain from completely abandoning its reformist WTL roots. Based on my collection of writing assignments, there is still much work to be done in order to make instructors across the curriculum aware of the benefits of expressive and poetic writing and the value of assignments that are written for audiences beyond the teacher-as-examiner.

Despite the ubiquity of exam writing, I did find it hopeful that a significant number of instructors responded to drafts, and that a substantial percentage of the assignments were exploratory journals. I believe this is a reflection of the influence of the WAC movement on the instructors in my study. The fact that the twelve courses in my study associated with a WAC initiative stood out for the variety of rhetorical situations the assignments presented to students, as well as the emphasis the WAC instructors placed on responding to drafts with more sophisticated roles than simply examiners looking for a correct answer, provides evidence of life in an otherwise bleak universe of college discourse. WAC courses were also notable because of the variety of disciplinary genres assigned, a point I will discuss further in the next chapter, where I consider the repeated rhetorical situations—the genres—of the writing assignments in my study.

3
SOCIAL ACTION, SOCIAL INACTION
The Genres of College Writing

The discussion in chapter 2 of the rhetorical situations in the 2,101 writing assignments I collected provided a sense of the primary purposes and audiences students are asked to write for in academic discourse. I discussed the ways instructors in my study utilized mostly limited purposes and audiences in their writing assignments, with the exception of courses connected to a Writing Across the Curriculum (WAC) initiative. But focusing primarily on purpose and audience only begins to tell the story of college writing, and in the chapters that follow I broaden the context of my analysis to rhetorical situations that have become typified through repetition (genres) and the broader contexts in which those genres operate (discourse communities).

In their longitudinal studies of college writing at Harvard and Stanford, Sommers and Saltz (2004) and Fishman et al. (2005) comment on the variety of genres students are asked to compose in. Previous surveys of the genres assigned in courses across the curriculum (Bridgeman and Carlson 1984; Eblen 1983; Harris and Hult 1985) have shown that instructors claim to assign a variety of genres, both academic and professional, but two genres remain dominant: the term paper and the short-answer exam. My results are similar to previous studies in that a variety of genres are assigned. Lab reports, executive summaries, book reviews, ethnographies, feasibility reports, essay exams, abstracts, annotated bibliographies, editorials, case

DOI: 10.7330/9780874219401.c003

studies, court briefs, company profiles, press releases, literature reviews—the list is truly extensive. There is, in fact, such
a variety of genres—and such a difference in the way those
genres are defined in their various disciplinary contexts—that
I will resist the urge to classify, or merely categorize genres by
their formal features and distribution. As genre studies theorists argue, genres are impossible to deduce from the structure
of the discourse act itself (Bazerman and Paradis 1991; Devitt
2008; Miller 1994; Prior 1998; Swales 1990). Rather than imposing static categories on dynamic uses of language by classifying
genres by formal features, my aim is to get a sense of the rhetorical context of the genres in my study. These contexts include
the purposes and audiences for genres, their social exigencies,
and how they vary from discipline to discipline and instructor to
instructor. In order to do this, I focus on the two genres found
to be the most common in previous surveys of college writing:
researched writing labeled "term papers" or "research papers,"
and the short-answer exam. These are also the most common
genres in my study.

RESEARCH PAPERS AND TERM PAPERS: THE
GENRE OF RESEARCHED WRITING

Writing in 1991, David Russell says, "One can only guess how
widely term papers were (or are) assigned, in what disciplines,
in what types of institutions, and at what levels. There has
never been a national survey of the term paper in the disciplines" (Russell 1991, 88). One reason I focus on the genre of
the research paper/term paper (from now on referred to as
research paper) is to address this gap in the research. Another
is because it is representative of almost all of the genres I
found in my research: it is too varied to classify by formal features, and too discipline-specific and even classroom-specific
to be considered as a type of writing, without also analyzing its
social context.

Prior to conducting this research, I was in agreement with
Russell's assertion that the genre of the research paper "has

come to be ubiquitous, relatively uniform, and almost syn-
onymous with extended school writing" (Russell 1991, 78).
Considering how common research papers were in prior surveys of college writing, and considering current stereotypes
about the uniformity of the college research paper, I expected
to find a significant number of research paper assignments in
my study, and I expected them to be similar in terms of purpose, audience, and form. Although there is a predominance
of writing assignments labeled "research paper" or "term
paper" by the instructors, the researched writing assignments
in my study had little in common in terms of genre conventions. Based on this, I agree with Richard Larson's (1982) argument that the research paper cannot be classified as a genre,
since research writing varies to such a degree from discipline
to discipline and from instructor to instructor. Prior surveys
that have used the label "research paper" or "term paper" do
so artificially, as a too convenient way to classify a broad range
of research writing.

Despite the variety of research papers in my study, I did find
a pattern in the writing that I think warrants at least one broad
distinction. Robert Davis and Mark Shadle divide research
papers into two categories: modernist and alternative (Davis
and Shadle 2000). The modernist research paper is the "traditional" research paper. It's informative in purpose, logical, thesis-driven, and objective. The purpose of a modernist research
paper is "not making knowledge so much as reporting the
known" (423). Modernist research papers, Davis and Shadle
argue, are "cliched and templated," and value "detachment,
expertise, and certainty" (417).

The instructions for one research paper in a biology course
echoed Davis and Shadle's conception of modernist research
papers: "Your papers should reflect your knowledge and understanding of what other scholars have said about your topic." A
British literature instructor did not want his students "to argue
a thesis or interpret the poem." The emphasis was on reporting
prior knowledge, not creating new knowledge. This instructor
focused on correct documentation, which is another aspect of

the modernist research paper, and he warned students, "I will penalize your paper severely if it is not adequately documented."

A research paper from a psychology course contained many of the features Davis and Shadle would call "modernist":

RESEARCH PAPER GUIDELINES

Purpose: The purpose of this project is for the student to 1) become familiar with a particular area of research activity in the field of human development, 2) by learning referencing techniques for this discipline, 3) gleaning information from the primary psychological literature, 4) summarizing this information clearly in a written report, and 5) practicing the format of scientific writing in this discipline.

Format: The format of the paper is a term paper about research, not an original research report. Each paper presents a summary of a single article.

Evaluation: The grade is based on content and form, including: Organization of the paper as a whole and of each section, adequacy of the summaries and interpretations of literature, the explication of controversial issues when appropriate, your conclusions and defense of your conclusions, grammar, punctuation, neatness, listing and citing of bibliographic references.

The grade will be lowered 10 points for each of the following:

errors in citation format

errors in reference format

failure to use APA format

excessive spelling, grammatical or punctuation errors

inaccurate information

This is a "term paper," not an "original research report." Students merely "glean" and "summarize" information. The evaluation criteria focus mainly on the correctness of information, citations, and grammar.

Perhaps a religious studies instructor provides the best description of the way alternative research writing differs from the modernist research paper. In a handout on writing essays, this instructor wrote:

> Remember when you were in grade six and your teacher told you to write a report on such and such or so and so, and you went to the library, opened up the encyclopedia, and tried to put the information into your own words? You should be past that now. A university essay is not a standard report that uses a few more books!

Alternative research writing values the creation of new knowledge, and not just "amassing of brute facts" (Connors 1997, 321). Alternative research writing values exploration and originality, and is often written in "poststructural" genres, such as ethnography or hypertext.

Compositionists have bemoaned the staying power of the traditional research paper, so I fully expected the majority of the research writing in my collection to fit in with Davis and Shadle's (2000) modernist category. I was instead surprised to find that the religious studies instructor was right: the majority of college research writing is closer in spirit to alternative rather than modernist. Take, for example, this research project from a psychology course:

Integration Project: As an integration course, cross-cultural psychology seeks to involve students in exploring the interrelationships between two or more disciplines. The purpose of the project is to help you do just that. The format of the project is open to your creative ideas as long as the project looks at culture from two or more disciplinary perspectives. Some options might be:

- A cross-cultural comparison on some topic of interest in psychology as well as another discipline (e.g. family structure, ceremonies and/or rituals, child rearing practices, delinquency, artistic expression, mental health, religiosity, therapy). Discuss how cross-cultural differences and similarities would be viewed and handled from the perspectives of a psychologist and a professional from the other field.

- A report of the cross-cultural psychological observations you made in a place where you had exposure to another culture (e.g. a church, a theater, a refugee center, an office) while being involved in an activity/job related to other disciplines (e.g. religion, art, social work, business administration).

- A critique of your own major or minor field of study (if you are not a psychology major or minor) from the point of view of cross-cultural psychology. You might discuss how inclusive and culturally sensitive the field of study is, citing specific research and theoretical examples.

- An analysis of a movie, a piece of music, or some literature from another culture. Using our textbook information, explain how the concepts in the text are depicted in the piece you are analyzing and/or how the piece can be explained by some of the concepts in the text.

The goal of this research project was not to report the known, but to encourage exploration, synthesis, and creativity. Students chose from a variety of genres, all of which required analysis, argument, or evaluation.

Another example of an alternative research project comes from a sociology course:

FINAL PROJECTS

There are two options for the final project, individual projects that deepen your understanding of the social movement you have been analyzing in your class papers, and collective projects that examine a new case (either the World Trade Organization protest or the "death with dignity" movement) to broaden you understanding of the theoretical questions we have examined. Individuals who choose the first option will be expected to write a longer research paper tying together the shorter exploratory papers into a tighter argument and adding to it by examining more documents or more secondary literature.

Further tips:

There are many ways to write a sociology paper. Judging from your papers this semester, all of you have an intuitive grasp of the elements of a good social science project. For those of you who would like a checklist, the following describes the elements sociologists try to incorporate into their papers:

1. A puzzle or question and the context that makes it theoretically interesting (e.g., something like Morris's questions about why black churches were so important to as nodes of mobilization for the civil rights movement, Gaventa's question about why, in a situation of extreme exploitation, Appalachians don't rebel, or Ferree and Hess's more implicit question about how social structural and political opportunities interacted to create the possibility for the emergence of a "new" feminist movement in the 1970s).

2. Review of two general sociological theories (e.g., in our case, theories of social movement behavior)

3. Discussion of at least two opposing topical explanations presented by area specialists you locate through your own library research on the movement

4. The argument you plan to evaluate and how you will do so (e.g., will you reexamine old evidence in light of a new theory? Will you examine new evidence that you discovered while conducting your document analysis?)

5. A conclusion in which you explain what further research would need to focus on, followed by a list of references

Most of you have been adhering to this model in your papers, and for your final projects, you should simply add further depth to your existing discussions that you began

> in your previous papers (e.g., whereas earlier papers were
> each around five pages, the final paper should be 10–15
> pages in length, excluding reference lists and any other
> appendices).

The goal of this research project was not to report the known,
but to "deepen" and "broaden" the students' own understanding. Students began with "a puzzle or a question." This project
introduced students to a disciplinary writing, which requires
more than just a mere amassing of facts.

Most of the research paper instructions in the study echo the
psychology assignment's insistence on exploration and argument, as these passages illustrate:

> The goal of the project is to provide you with an opportunity to
> integrate, synthesize, and apply the material we are studying in
> class in a real-world context, gain experience with group deci-
> sion making, research a topic in greater depth, and connect with
> a larger community.

> The purpose of this paper is to stimulate your thinking about
> "social or distributive justice." You are to develop you own posi-
> tion on this topic. Specifically, what principles should guide gov-
> ernment in determining what to guarantee its citizens.

> You'll begin to create your corporate portfolio by writing a
> corporate mission statement and corporate profile or image bro-
> chure, and you'll also begin to research the cross-cultural com-
> munication differences you uncover in your case. Next, you'll
> collaborate to write a consulting report. The report must identify
> the international, cross-cultural communication problems in the
> case (supporting your conclusions with research), identify pos-
> sible solutions to the primary problems (after comparing and
> contrasting the possibilities), and propose a solution to the
> appropriate audience (i.e., offer recommendations, and offer an
> implementation plan, and reasons).

As I began to collect writing assignments from across disciplines, I hypothesized that the traditional, modernist research
paper would be the dominant college research genre. The fact

that most of the researched writing in the study asked students to create knowledge and perform the meaning-making work of the discipline was a pleasant surprise, and a finding of importance to WAC practitioners and composition instructors, as I discuss in the conclusion of this chapter.

SHORT-ANSWER EXAMS: GENRE AS SOCIAL (IN)ACTION

Despite the apparent variety of genres in my study, and despite the variety of social contexts for writing from discipline to discipline and instructor to instructor, it's important to note that nearly a quarter of the assignments in my research were of the genre most lacking in rhetorical and social context: the short-answer exam. Although I try to avoid classifying genres by their formal features, perhaps short-answer exams are the one genre that resists the application of current genre theory and its emphasis on context and disciplinarity. As I collected and analyzed the assignments, the sheer force of exam writing became the most noticeable pattern in my research. A midterm and final exam is the only writing assigned in one out of every four courses, and as genres these exams show little variation across disciplines. They almost always consist of questions that require rote memorization and recall of facts, and the instructor consistently plays the role of teacher-as-examiner, looking for correct answers. The short-answer exam is the genre with the least "social action," to use Carolyn Miller's (1994) term. WID theorists are right to insist on looking at genres in their social context, but it is unfortunately the genre with the least social context that dominates my research.

One pattern I noticed in both short-answer and essay exams is the extraordinarily broad scope of questions that are supposed to be answered in a few sentences or—in the case of in-class essays—an hour or less. This fifty-minute American history exam is representative:

Write on one of the following two questions:

1) It is argued by some that the Soviet-American Cold War from 1947 through 1991 was inevitable given the results of World

War II and the ideological conflict between the two countries. Evaluate that argument.

2) Discuss the impact of American liberal democratic values on American national security policy during the Cold War.

In another American history course, students had one hour to answer four in-class exam questions, each of which could be the subject of a dissertation in history:

Discuss the evolution of the American Republic from 1782–1789.

Discuss the ratification of the Constitution and the forces the promoted its adoption.

Discuss the expansion of the United States from 1800–1850.

Discuss the developments and events that led to America's Civil War.

The short-answer exam questions from a global environment course also present students with an overwhelming task. In only a few sentences, students need to answer, "What is the environment?" "How does science work?" and "What is economics?" Perhaps this is one reason the word "exam" has negative connotations for most students—a fact that a gothic literature instructor implied when he said of his exams: "We inflict two."

RETHINKING GENRE IN COLLEGE WRITING

Research in genre theory (Bazerman and Paradis 1991; Devitt 2008; Miller 1994; Prior 1998; Swales 1990) has turned our attention to genres as dynamic social actions that can only be understood in the context of purpose, audience, and discourse community. This richer understanding of how genres work, an understanding that moves us beyond formal features and rigid rules, is certainly a useful lens for thinking about the many research papers in my collection. Given the ubiquity of "alternative" forms of researched writing in my study, and the relative lack of "modernist" research writing (Davis and Shadle 2000), I believe we need to rethink our assumptions about the way the research paper is assigned outside of composition courses.

Prior to conducting this research, as a WAC program coordinator I felt compelled to offer faculty development workshops on alternatives to the traditional research paper, with the premise that most faculty would come to these workshops assigning modernist research papers and leave with ideas for alternatives to the traditional. My research leads me to believe that the research paper genre is one of the most complex and dynamic genres in college writing, and one that instructors assign as a tool to encourage students to think critically, to introduce them to the ways of thinking in their discipline, and to prepare them for the workforce. For WAC practitioners, research genres may well be a point of leverage to reinforce best practices of faculty teaching genre as social action. For composition instructors, breaking students of the stereotype of research papers as modernist report writing and giving them practice with alternative research writing will help prepare them for the kinds of extended and sophisticated research genres they are likely to encounter in their disciplines.

Despite the value of alternative research writing genres, my study may force us to rethink the possibly generous view of students' experiences with genres across the curriculum held by WAC and genre theorists. We in WAC may endorse disciplinary genres as social action, and argue for the need to see genres as tools for initiating students to academic discourse communities in ways that prepare them to think like psychologists, engineers, biologists, and so on, but the reality of students' genre experience in college writing may be starker than we believe. Yes, there is an incredible variety of disciplinary and professional genres in my study, but the genre that dominates is the genre with the least social action. It is also the genre that does the least amount of work when introducing students to their disciplines, and rarely asks for critical thinking or consideration of an audience beyond the teacher-as-examiner.

As I culled through the assignments in my research, I was overwhelmed by the amount of short-answer and essay exams, and the limited view of academic thinking and writing these exam genres represent. Students taking the courses in my study are quite simply barraged with exams. Both WTL and WID theorists would see this dominance of exams as highly problematic, but for different reasons. WTL theorists would rightly bemoan the dominance of a genre that leaves no room for personal connection or writing as exploration. WID theorists would be disappointed to find that the most prevalent genre is the one that benefits students the least in terms of introducing them to ways of making meaning and entering them into the conversation of various discourse communities. Once again, the results of my research speak to the need for WAC practitioners to retain a reformist approach to faculty development, at least by helping instructors find alternatives to the genre of the short-answer exam.

4
EACH COURSE IS A COMMUNITY
The Discourse Communities of College Writing

In the discussion of genre in chapter 3, I expanded my analysis of the writing assignments in my study beyond just the rhetorical situation of purpose and audience, and considered the social action of typified rhetorical situations—the genres of college writing. But a complete analysis of writing genres must move into even broader contexts for making meaning in the disciplines. In college writing, genres do not stand in isolation, apart from the context of wider disciplines and sub-disciplines. Genre theorists argue that genres are constituted by and, at the same time, help to constitute discourse communities (Bawarshi 2000; Miller 1994; Swales 1990). As Swales says, "genres belong to discourse communities, not to individuals" (9). In this chapter, then, I move beyond genre and discuss what the writing assignments in my research reveal about the discourse communities of academic disciplines as well as the broader discourse community of academic writing in the United States. I explore two primary questions: Is there such a thing as "academic writing"? And in what ways are expectations for writing similar and different across courses in the same discipline?

To define the concept "discourse community," I rely on the seminal work of John Swales (1990), who posits that a discourse community has the following qualities:

- A discourse community has a broadly agreed set of common public goals.

DOI: 10.7330/9780874219401.c004

- A discourse community has mechanisms of intercommunication among its members.
- A discourse community uses its participatory mechanisms primarily to provide information and feedback.
- A discourse community utilizes and hence possesses one or more genres in the communicative furtherance of its aims.
- In addition to owning genres, a discourse community has acquired some specific lexis.
- A discourse community has a threshold level of members with a suitable degree of relevant content and discoursal experience. (24–27)

With Swales's definition in mind, I ask of the assignments in my research: Is there a broadly shared set of goals across all the assignments, or within specific disciplines? Are there shared academic genres across and/or within disciplines? What discoursal experience is needed to be a successful academic writer? These are some of the questions I explore in this chapter.

"THE FORMAL ESSAY": ACADEMIC DISCOURSE AS GENERIC

Judy Gill feels that "there in fact exists something we can call generic academic writing standards and expectations that are cross- or trans-disciplinary" (Gill 1996, 166). A number of scholars have posited, like Gill, that it's possible to broadly define the values and expectations of college writing. Michael Pemberton, reflecting upon academic writing and the role of the writing center, argues that

> some 'transdisciplinary' textual or rhetorical features also exist, features that might be addressed successfully by tutors in a writing center. The need to support generalizations with specific evidence, for example, may display some subtle variations depending upon the discipline and audience addressed in particular texts, but the fact that there must be *some* relationship between generalizations made and evidence offered in support is a feature common to virtually all academic writing. (Pemberton 1995, 118)

Chris Thaiss and Terry Myers Zawacki echo Gill and Pemberton's assertion that transdisciplinary academic writing features do exist on a broad level (2006). In their research into academic writing at George Mason University, Thaiss and Zawacki found that, for both students and faculty, there are features of academic writing that cut across disciplines. These features include, "clear evidence in writing that the writer(s) have been persistent, open-minded, and disciplined in study," "the dominance of reason over emotion or sensual perception," and "an imagined reader who is coolly rational, reading for information, and intending to formulate a reasoned response" (5–7). Thaiss and Zawacki also found "an overwhelming amount of commonness of an array of terms such as 'evidence,' 'organized,' and 'grammar'" (88).

Qualities such as rational inquiry, evidence from research, and clear and grammatically correct writing are presented as features of college writing throughout Patrick Sullivan and Howard Tinberg's *What is "College-Level" Writing?* In the first chapter of the book, Sullivan defines academic writing as:

- A willingness to evaluate ideas and issues carefully
- Some skill at analysis and higher-level thinking
- The ability to shape and organize material effectively
- The ability to integrate some of the material from the readings skillfully
- The ability to follow the standard rules of grammar, punctuation, and spelling. (Sullivan and Tinberg 2006, 17)

In his faculty development guide, *Engaging Ideas*, John Bean echoes Thaiss and Zawacki and Sullivan and Tinberg in his assertion that there are qualities of critical thinking that cross disciplines: challenging assumptions, engaging in dialogue, and providing evidence to support arguments (2011, 4). Mark Waldo found shared criteria for good writing in learning outcomes statements from various departments at the University of Nevada, Reno. The values he found that cut across disciplines include critical thinking, error-free writing, and writing clearly (2003, 151).

Other scholars have approached the shared values and expectations of academic writing by asserting that there are shared rhetorical "moves" that academic writers make, and that these moves should be taught in explicit ways. David Bartholomae (1986), Graff and Birkenstein (2009), Joseph Harris (2006), and John Swales (1990) have noted that academic writers, no matter what their discipline, make moves such as citing previous expert knowledge on the topic, pointing to a gap in that knowledge, making arguments that counter commonplaces about a subject, and applying theories in new contexts to create new knowledge.

It appears that the two features most composition scholars associate with college writing are systematic research and the integration of evidence—analysis, argument, and problem solving in service of addressing gaps in the literature, clarity and organization, and grammatical correctness. The question for my own research, then, is whether or not these broad criteria for college writing were reflected across the writing assignments in my study. On the surface, the answer is yes.

A distinct pattern in my research is the repeated appearance of a kind of generic, archetypal structure that instructors simply refer to as "the formal essay." This almost templated form of essay writing is discussed in strikingly similar ways in assignments across the curriculum, as is evident in these passages from assignment descriptions in history, religious studies, and sociology courses:

> Your paper should follow the conventions of formal essay writing. There should be an introductory paragraph stating the thesis or organizing principle of the paper, several paragraphs supporting the main idea in the introduction, and a concluding paragraph that sums up what has gone before.

> Each essay should have a solid thesis statement in the introduction, should follow formal essay guidelines (introduction, body, conclusion), and should be carefully written to avoid grammatical and spelling errors.

> In order to write a good essay you need to develop a thesis. The first paragraph briefly outlines the issue your paper addresses

then presents a clearly formulated thesis statement. The final
paragraph simply summarizes what you have demonstrated.

In the introduction give the reader an overview of your essay,
then in each paragraph address one of the main ideas included
in the outline. In the conclusion remind the reader of how the
ideas are related.

Sullivan argues that one feature of college-level writing is "the
ability to shape and organize material effectively" (Sullivan and
Tinberg 2006, 17). Based on the formulaic structure of the
academic essay, as described by the instructors in my research,
the definition of "effective" organization is not as complex and
sophisticated as those who have written about the shared features of academic writing might have led us to believe. The
instructors define the academic essay as rhetorically narrow
compared to the writing in their own scholarly work.

Although this generic academic essay is common in my
collection of writing assignments, there are times when the
students are asked to break from the formula: when they
are assigned extended research projects; when they write for
exploratory purposes in journals; or when they write in a specific disciplinary genre, such as the lab report, court brief, or
business plan. This research leads me to believe in a paradox
concerning academic writing: that there is such a thing as a
generic, academic essay, but there are also enough cases of students being asked to break from this formulaic essay that it is
more useful to think of academic writing as discipline-specific
instead of reducing it to generic features. Richard Coe (2001)
argues, ". . . we should destabilize the reductive conceptions
of school genres as rigid text formats, which our students typically bring to our classes, especially in relation to the pedagogical genres known as the *research paper . . . the essay . . .* and *the
paragraph*" (198). I would argue that we need to do two things
at once: make students aware that there are some instructors
across disciplines who will present them with formulaic, rigid
versions of the "research paper," "the essay," and "the paragraph," but also inform them of the fact that most research
papers they will write, most essays they will be assigned, and

most paragraphs they will develop will be situated in rhetorical situations, genres, and discourse communities.

AN OBSESSION WITH CORRECTNESS

Where there is no paradox and almost complete agreement among instructors across academic writing disciplines is the high value placed on grammatical correctness. For many instructors in my research, an essay free of grammatical errors was a minimum, baseline requirement. One American studies instructor told her students: "I will expect correct grammar and spelling as a baseline, and will not assign a grade to papers that do not meet this baseline. (You can resubmit these once you have fixed them, but they can only receive a minus)." This attitude was repeated in a business writing instructor's course description: "An assignment is acceptable only when it contains no typographical errors or misspellings and when all grammar, punctuation, format, and information (names, dates, titles, etc.) are correct." A Chinese economy instructor said of his fifteen-page research paper: "At a minimum, your writing should be free of spelling errors and grammar errors." For these instructors, correctness, not content, is the fundamental requirement of writing—a requirement even found in timed writing as well. In his assignment description for an in-class essay test, a business administration instructor wrote: "Your papers are expected to be well organized, legible and free of any grammatical or spelling mistakes. If you need to, bring a dictionary with you." Although Thaiss (1998) argues that many teachers outside English don't comment on errors because they lack the time or confidence to find them, the instructors in my research seemed to have both the will and the time to hunt for mistakes.

This focus on grammatical correctness often causes instructors, who are also focusing on content, to make higher order concerns seem like an afterthought, as is evident in assignment descriptions and writing guides. Under "Grading" in a term paper description for a business law course, the instructor mentioned the aspects of writing that can affect point totals, amounting to a list of surface errors: verb tense changes, misspelled words, incorrect citations, etc. After this long list of errors to avoid, the instructor wrote: "Please offer analysis, also." In the "How to Write Papers" section of a criminal justice syllabus, the instructor warned students: "Do not permit examples of the following in your paper," and gave a long list of common grammar errors. The students' grades "will be based on the above criteria, plus organization, content, clarity, and usage." Content took a back seat in the list of grammar mistakes, and "usage" was further emphasized. Nearly half of the assignments that mentioned evaluation criteria gave this kind of emphasis to correctness.

John Bean states, "When teachers across disciplines complain that students 'haven't learned to write,' they often think first of sentence-level errors" (2011, 66). Often the instructors in my research equated writing itself with correctness. The instructor of a European history course wrote:

> Since this is the final paper in a writing course, I'll be looking closely at your writing and the improvement you've made. If you have had problems with inappropriate word choices, I'll expect to see more precise vocabulary. If I have been marking your commas all semester . . . well, I'm sure you get the idea.

If students don't get the idea, it will most likely be emphasized in their other courses. For example, an art history course, where the section on "writing" in the course description contains only a single sentence: "Grammatical and structural correctness, accurate spelling, and clean copy are expected." A psychology instructor appears to separate thinking and writing. He wrote: "Evaluation will be based on demonstrated understanding of the psychological concepts involved in the research . . . and your writing, including spelling, grammar, use of complete sentences, etc."

Considering this equating of writing with correctness, it's not surprising that instructors sometimes view campus writing centers as places to edit writing. An environmental studies instructor told students:

> I expect good, coherent reports, free of spelling mistakes and grammatical errors. Please use the spelling checker that comes with your word processor! Even then, you must still proofread! Take advantage of the many support services on campus, particularly the Writing Center.

A different environmental instructor told students that answers to exams "should be in complete, grammatically correct sentences. All words should be correctly spelled. If you need help you should go to the Reading, Writing, and Study Skills Lab." A public speaking instructor associated correctness with composition for English classes in general, stating that "writing assignments will be given and will be graded with the same scrutiny received in an English class. Proofread!"

In chapter 2, I discussed the mixed signals students are given concerning purpose and audience, and instructors in my research gave similar mixed signals about content and correctness. For example, an American history instructor informed students that "the three most common types of comments I make on student writing involve either; 1) failing to clearly address the topic; 2) failing to give enough concrete and persuasive evidence; or 3) failing to adequately explain how the facts given advance your argument." This statement was directly followed by a section titled "Writing Tips" that discussed only errors of usage, grammar, and capitalization. A human growth and development instructor emphasized her grading of term papers on content and not just form, but also that "the grade will be lowered ten points for each of the following: errors in citation format, errors in reference format, failure to use APA format, or excessive spelling, grammatical, or punctuation errors." Another instructor gave a similar kind of mixed message about creativity vs. correctness in the "formal essay":

> Have a classmate or friend read over your paper for grammatical or spelling errors. Write an outline, and work from there. You should have an introduction which outlines what you talk about, one or two of your major points, and a one-sentence suggestion on how you will close your essay. Let things flow.

It would certainly be difficult for many of the students in my research to "let things flow," considering many instructors' emphasis on sentence-level correctness.

THE DIVERSITY OF ACADEMIC DISCOURSE COMMUNITIES

In their study of student and faculty writing across disciplines at George Mason University, Thaiss and Zawacki (2006) may have found broad shared criteria for academic writing and common terms used across disciplines, but they also discovered that "disciplines are much more fluid and elusive than programmatic names suggest" (13). Thaiss and Zawacki conclude that, despite some common features of academic writing that cut across disciplines, individual disciplines and even individual instructors within disciplines present students with extremely diverse criteria for writing. In his chapter in *WAC for the New Millennium*, Thaiss believes that WAC research should focus as much on "writing-in-the-course" as "writing-in-the-discipline" (1998, 324). In a sense, Thaiss is arguing that each course is its own discourse community. Waldo also found that although there were some broad writing criteria shared by departments at University of Nevada, Reno—criteria I mentioned earlier in this chapter—a close look at departmental learning outcomes revealed that "what makes writing good in one discipline certainly does not make it good in another" (2003, 6).

Thaiss's and Waldo's skepticism about defining "academic writing" in some singular fashion is shared by a number of prominent composition theorists. David Russell argues that academia is not "a single discourse community but a collection of discrete communities . . . each with its own specialized written discourse" (1991, 5). The boundaries of these communities, according to Michael Carter, are "porous and in flux" (2007, 410). In his seminal article on community in the study of writing, Joseph Harris claims, "The 'Academic Discourse Community' is a utopia, tied to no particular time or place" (1989, 14). Harris prefers the metaphor of a city rather than a community to reflect the diversity of college discourse community memberships.

My research also leads me to be skeptical about generalizing academic writing and academic disciplines. On the one hand, it's true that—like Thaiss and Zawacki—I found a very broad notion of what makes for good academic writing that seems to cross disciplines. However, looking deeper than the broadest and most formulaic sense of academic writing, I found vast differences across disciplines and even among instructors in the same discipline.

As a case in point, there is incredible disciplinary diversity within the genre "research paper" or "term paper." Although in chapter 3 I used Davis and Shadle's (2000) "modernist" and "alternative" categories in research writing as a way to make distinctions between two broad types of research writing in my study, a closer look at the research papers in my collection reveals a deeper truth about the genres in my study. The differences within and among disciplines —and even among instructors within the same discipline and sub-discipline—in terms of purpose, audience, research methods, what counts as evidence, how research papers are structured, and the persona the writer is asked to take on make it difficult to generalize about the research paper as an academic genre, just as it would be difficult to generalize about the "lab report" or the "journal" without considering both disciplinary and classroom contexts.

Consider, for example, what it means to conduct research and what counts as evidence in the researched writing in my study. A political science research project asked students to "research every aspect of the political background of the incumbent" for a presentation before the local Democratic Party organization. This required primarily textual research, and the instructor recommended that students do a thorough search of sources such as *Congressional Quarterly* and *The Almanac of American Politics.* The research had a public audience, and was required to be persuasive to Democratic Party insiders, who would have certain expectations for any research of this kind (e.g., the use of data from polls). In a political psychology course, also in the social sciences, the method of investigation for the research paper included "administering a questionnaire," "participant observation," and "database analysis," all of which require a different set of research skills and have different research expectations than the presentation to the local Democratic Party.

In an American history course, students are asked to approach research and evidence in a way that is different from the two social science courses. Students must "empathize with the person, place, or event you are writing about. The goal here is to use your understanding of the primary and secondary sources you have read to 'become' that person." This approach aligns with the instructor's notion that history is socially constructed: that "historians come to a socially negotiated understanding of historical figures and events" (a view of the way historical knowledge is created that is not always in accord with the views of other history instructors in my research, especially those that assign only short-answer exams). What counts as evidence in this history course is far more broadly defined than in the political science courses: "old family photos, a grandparent's memories, even family reunions allow people to understand their lives through an appreciation of the past." Evidence is explicitly connected to the discipline of history: "These events and artifacts remind us that history is a dynamic and interpretive field of study that requires far more than rote memorization."

Researched writing in the business courses in my study value research and evidence that is, as one business instructor put it, "quantitative and concise." Research and evidence in a marketing course means "a table with a frequency distribution with counts and percentages" as well as "at least three pages of chi-square analyses" and "one page of a correlation/regression analysis." Another business instructor advised students to "make your descriptions and analyses precise and factual. Specific data about costs, market shares, time to market, and so on will enrich your work. In other words, what do the numbers tell us?" Just as historical figures and artifacts told the story for the American history course, here numbers are the story. Despite the ubiquity of this emphasis on quantitative data, the form in which this research story is told differs dramatically from business course to business course. Business research genres in my study include executive summaries, proposals, business plans, case studies, progress reports, company profiles, and marketing campaigns—all of which use quantitative data in different contexts, for different purposes, and for different audiences. Thaiss's (1998) argument that WAC research should focus as much on writing within individual courses as writing in broader disciplines is typified in my analysis of the research paper as a genre.

At a more micro level than genre, consider the ways rhetorical strategies such as "evaluate," "argue," or "describe" differ across disciplines in the assignments in my study. It's impossible to speak of "arguing" or "describing" or "explaining" in general terms, since each discipline—and often different teachers in the same discipline—have a slightly different way of defining each of these strategies. As David Bartholomae argues, words such as "analyze, define, describe, argue . . . are located in a very specialized discourse. Analysis, for example, is a very different activity—its textual forms, that is, vary greatly—in an English course, a history course, a sociology course or a chemistry course" (Bartholomae 1983, 310).

In the humanities and social sciences courses in my research, "explaining" usually means explaining the meaning of an idea, position, theory, or event. An instructor of English literature asked students to "explain the meaning of a passage and how that meaning is conveyed. An informed explanation of the specific words on the page, not simply a summary of what the work itself is about and not a summary of the poet's ideas." In an assignment for an American government course, students had to "explain the principles of government identified in the text and in class as characterizing our system under the Constitution." The evidence to develop these explanations must come from the student's own ideas and the text. In the hard sciences and the social sciences, however, "explain" takes on a different meaning. In these disciplines, explaining often means using diagrams, charts, and tables to illustrate something "objectively." For example, in a geology assignment the instructor asked, "What types of faults are associated with fault block mountains? Draw a diagram that helps explain your answer." In an anthropology course, students were required to explain a hypothesis that's already been tested by scientists and "use tables to summarize data relations." To an English teacher, this kind of summarizing of data may appear dry or uncreative. But instructors in the sciences view a well-written table or chart the way an English instructor might view a well-written sentence or paragraph. As a forestry instructor said in his assignment sheet, "the explanation of the tables and graphs is where the data 'comes to life.'"

A similar difference between disciplines is true of the rhetorical strategy "analyze." In the sciences, analyzing usually means collecting, organizing, and assessing data. This sense of the term is made explicit in the list of objectives for a microbiology course. Under "analysis skills," the instructor wrote: "Collecting and organizing data in a systematic fashion, presenting data in an appropriate form, assessing the validity of the data, and drawing appropriate conclusions based on the results." A nutrition analysis assignment in an anthropology course asked students to "analyze food and servings (calories, protein, etc.) and create analysis comparisons via bar graphs." Business courses also associate analysis with charts and tables. An assignment in a marketing research course required "chi-square and regression analysis," "tables and graphs," and "cross tabulations." A global economy instructor told students to "illustrate your analysis with at least five diagrams or tables from the OECD Economic Outlook."

"Analysis" in the humanities requires students to respond to ideas in texts and works of art, consider historical contexts, and theorize and make generalizations. In an "analysis essay" for a romantic literature course, the instructor asked: "To what extent is the biography of the writer necessary for a sound appreciation of the literature?" In an essay exam, a humanities instructor gave students a passage from Virgil with these instructions: "Using this passage as a point of departure, analyze the role and effects of omens, sacrifices, or rituals in the texts of

Virgil." This view of analysis is also reinforced in course objectives, where an art history instructor said that one major goal of the course was "analyzing the formal characteristics and subject matter of art works within their different historical contexts."

A similar kind of disciplinary difference is true of the strategy "describe." When instructors in business and the sciences ask students to "describe," they are most often asking for something akin to defining, summarizing, and explaining. Consider these examples from assignments in the hard sciences:

> Describe how you prepared the solution, including gram and mole amounts for your reagent.

> Describe what happens when you mix each of the reagents prepared in lab with Cl ion.

> Describe in detail the mechanisms that produce one of the following processes. Name all relevant structures or molecules involved. (A well- labeled diagram with explanatory remarks will do.)

> A description of the area visited. Include the type of rocks, name and age of the formations, and geologic processes which have affected the area.

> Describe your system design, implementation, testing, and analysis of how the different parameters you tested influence the performance of the scheduler.

In a business course assignment, students had to "describe how we measure inflation" and "Describe the gains to trade" for two countries. Two psychology instructors required students to "describe bottom-up and top-down approaches to perception" and "describe the research methods, major variables, and the study itself."

"Description" in the humanities is much more subjective, as this assignment from an art survey course illustrates:

> Describe the facade's formal character as fully and vividly as possible. You need not worry about researching the building's history or about using specialized architectural vocabulary. Just try to look, think, and describe with clarity, directness, precision, and vitality. Do you like or resent what the place is doing to you?

How is the building integrated into its immediate surroundings? Have your attitudes toward it changed with sustained looking?

Like the description required in business and science courses, description in the humanities often requires that students think analytically. But "vividly" and "vitality" are two keywords I didn't find in assignments in business or the sciences, and the questions at the end of this assignment point to the subjective nature of description in the humanities. This is seen again in an American studies assignment that asked students to "develop your own description of an early, familiar place. Describe it in detail, including as many senses and memories as seem meaningful. Respond in a very personal way."

The "comparison" rhetorical strategy illustrates another difference between the various disciplines. The majority of science and business assignments that ask students to make comparisons are operating at the comprehension level of Bloom's (1956) taxonomy. These assignments ask students to compare theories or data without requiring them to express their own opinions. The following examples illustrate this point:

Briefly discuss the main themes and concepts developed by these authors and then present a brief analysis of their similarities and differences in regard to methodology, vision of society, perception of the future, and other pertinent issues.

Compare and contrast processual and post-processual archaeologies.

How are property rights for forests different than those for fish?

How is economic profit different from accounting profit?

In humanities courses, students are usually required to express their own opinion on an issue after making comparisons, which moves the assignments up from the abstraction level in Bloom's scale and into the analysis, synthesis, and evaluation levels. A take-home essay exam from a humanities course illustrates this higher-level comparison:

Write a comparison of the "Homeric" version of Demeter & Persephone with Ovid's version. Note and briefly summarize the

episodes that the two versions have in common, the episodes
from the "Homeric" version that Ovid has omitted, and the
episodes that he has added to that version. Note the differences
in detail within the episodes that the two versions share (in reference to the characters, locations, descriptions, motives, etc.)

Finally give a critique of the Homeric and Ovidian treatments
that you have just compared descriptively. State the difference in
structure, style, tone, and emphasis. Which version do you like
better and why?

Similarly, a women's studies course assignment asked students
to "note commonalties and differences in women's experiences from different regions in the world. In addition, record
your thoughts and reactions to the readings." In a US history
essay assignment, the instructor asked: "What are the major
social and political similarities and differences among southern, northern, and middle colonies up to the mid-eighteenth
century? Which do you think is more important—their similarities or differences—in explaining the nature of these colonies."
Students begin these assignments by summarizing and making
comparisons, but end with a critique, where they offer their own
analysis and opinions.

Discourse community ways of thinking and writing, the purpose and structures of genres, and rhetorical strategies such as
"describing," "explaining," and "analyzing" vary both by discipline and by instructor in the assignments in my study. They
vary enough that my impression—after having closely looked
at over 2,000 writing assignments across disciplines—is that
academic writing is a term not be used loosely. At the broadest
level, we may be able to generalize about the traditional formal
academic essay, but we do so to the disservice of college students
who are just as likely to encounter more sophisticated and discipline-specific genres of research writing, or assignments that
are connected not to abstractions about what a specific discipline values, but rather to the specific criteria or rubric of the
individual instructor or assignment. Richard Haswell (1991)
warns that "setting the academic as a target style can be counter-
developmental even in the context of the academy," and this is

certainly the case when "the academic" is used as a generic style that allegedly crosses disciplines (183). Although a limitation of my research design is that it doesn't allow me to build theories about why discourse communities differ across disciplines, or understand how students respond to these disciplinary differences, the breadth of discoursal evidence I am able to collect does add to our growing sense of the complexity of students' experiences with academic writing.

WRITING TO LEARN, WRITING IN THE DISCIPLINES, AND ACADEMIC DISCOURSE COMMUNITIES

My finding regarding the paradox of the generic "formal essay" found across disciplines and the simultaneous diversity of expectations and genres among even instructors in the same discipline has implications for both "Writing to Learn" (WTL) and "Writing in the Disciplines" (WID) approaches to academic discourse. Both WTL and WID theorists would resist the generic formal academic essay, but for different reasons. WTL theorists would see the formal essay, with its emphasis on objectivity and logical structure, as a restrictive notion of college writing. They would be especially concerned with the ways that the emphasis on grammatical correctness might hinder students' writing processes and teach them that correctness is more important than the use of writing as a tool for learning and discovery. WID theorists would also be concerned about this obsession with correctness, but their concern might focus on the disconnect between what instructors claim they value and what they actually value in their grading rubrics and assignment descriptions.

Although WID theorists would be interested in my research's further confirmation that there are broad criteria that cross disciplines, most WID theorists, from Bazerman and Paradis (1991) to Herrington and Curtis (2000) to Russell (1991), are more interested in the specific ways that academic disciplines differ instead of the more generic ways they are similar. My findings about the variety of expectations for researched writing, and the ways each instructor's expectation connects to his or her disciplinary ways of thinking—especially the idea that even instructors in the same discipline have different conceptions of what is valued in researched writing—provide further evidence for WID theorists of the heterogeneity of academic discourse communities. Whether it's a composition course, a writing center tutoring session, or a WAC workshop, we simply cannot use terms like "analyze" or "argue" or "describe" in generic ways. "Analyze" means something entirely different in a business course than it does in an English course than it does in an anthropology course, and even two instructors teaching the same course in the same discipline could define analysis in completely different ways. As Judith Langer (1992) argues, "forms like comparison or summary can be discussed in general ways, but then the particular uses of those forms in particular disciplinary contexts is lost" (quoted in Herrington 1985, 85).

I will further discuss the implications of my findings regarding academic discourse communities, rhetorical situations, and genres in chapter 6. However, before considering those implications, I wish to focus on the twelve courses in my research that work against the trend of presenting students with limited rhetorical situations, narrow genres, and mixed messages regarding disciplinary discourse communities. These courses, the courses in my research connected to a WAC initiative, stand out to such a degree that they are worth looking more closely. I consider the rhetorical situations, genres, and notions of discourse communities in these twelve WAC courses in chapter 5.

5
THE POWER OF WRITING
ACROSS THE CURRICULUM
Writing Assignments in WAC Courses

Thus far the story of my research into writing assignments across the curriculum has been, for the most part, a story dominated by informative writing to the teacher-as-examiner, in the form of the short-answer exam. Although I've discussed some significant positive patterns across the 2,101 writing assignments in my collection—the valuing of alternative research writing, the strong presence of exploratory writing in the form of journals, the number of instructors who ask for drafts—overall the limited purposes and audiences for writing in my study are similar to the limited purposes and audiences found in studies of secondary school writing by Applebee (1984) and Britton et al. (1975) over two decades ago. My results might lead one to speculate that the WAC movement has had some influence on US college writing in the form of increased journal writing and more emphasis on writing as a process, but not enough of an influence to truly make a dent in the lecture/exam pedagogy that appears to dominate college teaching.

A closer look at the courses in this study, however, reveals a very different picture of the influence of the WAC movement. The instructors in my research who: 1) assign the widest variety of purposes, audiences, and genres; 2) consistently provide students with interesting and complex rhetorical situations, rather than just the traditional lecture/exam format; and 3) teach writing as a process through peer response or commenting on

DOI: 10.7330/9780874219401.c005

rough drafts are often teaching a course connected in some way to a WAC initiative. This might be a writing-intensive course, a team-taught course with an English department faculty member, a learning community, or a course connected to an adjunct tutoring program. Instructors from writing-intensive courses affiliated with established WAC programs at institutions such as University of Missouri-Columbia, Cornell, Duke, University of Minnesota, and Stanford assigned the most writing, asked students to write for the greatest variety of audiences in the greatest variety of genres, and adopted common WAC pedagogical tools such as journaling, free-writing, grading rubrics, and peer response. Although only a dozen of the courses in my research were explicitly connected to a WAC initiative, these courses represent a persuasive group of case studies of the influence of the WAC movement. Where WAC initiatives have become a formal part of the institutional culture—in the form of writing-intensive courses or writing fellows programs—the transformation of writing pedagogy is impressive.

Tables 5.1–5.4 reveal significant differences between the distribution of purposes and audiences for the WAC courses versus the rest of the courses in my research:

Table 5.1. Distribution of the purposes of writing for WAC courses

Purpose	Number of Assignments	Percentage of Total
Transactional (total)	60	70
Informative	43	49
Persuasive	17	21
Expressive	5	6
Exploratory	20	23
Poetic	2	Less than 1%

Table 5.2. Distribution of the purposes of writing for all courses

Purpose	Number of Assignments	Percentage of Total
Transactional (total)	1,751	83
Informative	1,399	66
Persuasive	352	17

Purpose	Number of Assignments	Percentage of Total
Expressive	62	3
Exploratory	279	13
Poetic	9	Less than 1%

Table 5.3. Distribution of the audiences for writing in WAC courses

Audience	Number of Assignments	Percentage of Total
Student to Examiner	35	40
Student to Instructor (general)	13	15
Peers	5	6
Self	18	21
Wider Audience	16	18

Table 5.4. Distribution of the audiences for writing in all courses

Audience	Number of Assignments	Percentage of Total
Student to Examiner	1,343	64
Student to Instructor (general)	388	18
Peers	117	6
Self	111	5
Wider Audience (total)	142	7
Informed	89	4
Novice	29	2
Generalized Reader	24	1

Only half of the transactional writing assigned in the subset of WAC courses was writing to inform, compared to 66 percent in the sample at large. Instructors in WAC courses assigned twice as much expressive writing as the other instructors in my research. Sixty-four percent of the assignments in the overall sample had the audience of teacher-as-examiner, but 40 percent of WAC course assignments were written for an examiner audience. Only 5 percent of the instructors in my research asked students to reflect on their learning in assignments written for the audience of the self, but 21 percent of the WAC instructors assigned writing for the self. WAC instructors were more than twice as likely to ask students to write for wider audiences beyond the instructor, and assigned significantly more writing as well. The average number of writing assignments per course overall was 5.25, but the average number of writing assignments per WAC course was 8.7.

To get a clear sense of just how impressive the dozen WAC courses in my study are, I want to take a closer look at the writing assigned as well as the ways these WAC instructors discuss writing in their assignments, syllabi, grading rubrics, and other course materials such as writing guides. The following are the WAC courses in my study that I will be discussing in this chapter:

Agricultural Economics 183, University of Missouri, Columbia

BIO 310: Evolution, University of Nevada

Biology 108: Genetics and Society, University of Missouri, Columbia

SOM310: Management Communication, University of Massachusetts

BUSN2030: Business English and Communications, Utah State University Eastern

CLST11S.01: Greek Civilization, Duke

Economics 101: The Economics of Climate Change, Stanford

ENST495: Senior Seminar in Environmental Studies, Keene State College

HIST100.81: Intolerance and the Birth of Europe, Cornell

HIST3151: History of the British Isles, University of Minnesota

S49 Philosophy 4: Critical Thinking, DeAnza Community College

W2000: Writing in the Business World, Fort Lewis College

These courses are all either part of a writing-intensive program, a WID focus, or connected to an adjunct tutoring program for writing.

The pedagogy of these WAC courses is strikingly similar— enough so that I can make some generalizations about the writing assignments in these courses:

- WAC course assignments include self-reflective writing.
- WAC course assignments are often written to wider audiences beyond the teacher.

- WAC course assignments include alternative, discipline-specific researched writing projects, rather than midterms and final exams.
- Disciplinary genres and ways of thinking are made explicit in WAC course assignments.
- WAC course assignments usually require drafting, revising, and peer response.

I use these five generalizations to organize the rest of this chapter. I provide specific examples from assignments to support my argument that, in contrast to many of the lecture- and exam-focused courses in my research, these WAC courses present students with diverse and rhetorically rich composing situations and processes, and introduce them to the work of academic discourse communities through an explicit introduction to disciplinary genres and ways of thinking.

WAC COURSE ASSIGNMENTS INCLUDE SELF-REFLECTIVE WRITING

One of the most striking contrasts in my research is between the amount of writing to the audience of the self in WAC courses compared to my sample as a whole. Only 5 percent of the 2,101 writing assignments in my collection were self-reflective, compared to 21 percent of the WAC assignments. In other words, *most* of the assignments written for the self in the 400 courses I researched were found in these twelve WAC courses.

The self-reflective writing assignments in the WAC courses exemplify the ways instructors integrated WTL and WID approaches. Often, instructors asked students to think about their own history in order to make personal connections to their career choices. The personal and professional are integrated in the mission statement assignment from SOM310: Management Communication:

PERSONAL MISSION STATEMENT

Write an essay describing your background and experience, and the personal and business values you hold, values that have developed out of your unique background, training, and education. Your essay should concisely present your professional career goals, beginning with graduation and extending out for 5 years, and should help the reader understand how your background and important influences in your life (people or events) have led to your current focus. At the end of the piece, your reader should have a good sense of where you are headed professionally.

Self-evaluations are a common type of self-reflective writing, and in SOM310 the instructor explicitly connects self-assessment and the work of business professionals in a self-evaluation for a team project:

> Describe and assess your communication performance during the team project, *writing as if you were a supervisor of the training division who must evaluate the oral and written communication skills of team members throughout the company.* Focus on offering feedback on your own part of the project, but from this supervisory perspective. Try to be objective, and neutral or positive, rather than overly critical or defensive. (This assignment asks you to write a "mock" performance appraisal, as a way of arriving at a self-evaluation.)
>
> Note your strengths, especially noting aspects that might lead to promotion, and offer ways to build on these strengths. Then, offer specific recommendations for improvement, and note any aspects that were missing. Write "as if" this memo would be placed in the (your) employee file. Conclude the memo with specific recommendations for further growth, and/or for promotion. If you observe weaknesses that must be addressed because they could interfere with future performance, offer an improvement plan.

This kind of connection between personal reflection and the work of a discipline or profession is common in the WAC courses in my research. When WAC instructors ask students to reflect on their personal histories or make personal connections to what they were reading in class, they do so in order to further students' subject knowledge. This "Purpose and Context" assignment from S49 Philosophy 4 is representative:

> For this assignment (worth 15 points) you will write a 3 to 5 page typed, (1.5 or double-spaced) "Purpose and Context" paper.
>
> In this paper you will try to express to me and to yourself:
>
> 1) At this point in your life, what are your future goals? (i.e.,—what sort of life do you wish for yourself; what sort of life are you aiming for?). It's up to you whether the goals you choose are short term—in the next five years or long term or both. Your goals should be as concrete and specific as possible.
>
> 2) How do the following social factors influence or shape the goal(s) you just mentioned?
>
> Don't be hard on yourself if you feel a bit confused by this; few of us have been asked to do this in our lives, at least formally in writing. Think of this paper as a beginning, as an opportunity to see the relationship between where you've been and where you intend to go in your life.
>
> For the purpose of this paper I define personal history as the history of your life and the influences on your life. Ten factors are listed below. You must discuss the asterisked factors (there are seven). You may of course discuss all 10.
>
> You can organize the paper however you wish just as long as it's clear to me the social factor being discussed and its relationship to your goals. Thus I will grade you according to three criteria: 1) Do you mention clearly at least six factors (with the asterisks)? 2) Do you provide

a **suggestive causal explanation** from each social factor to your goals? (If there truly is none then briefly say why there is no causal relationship); 3) is your writing relatively clear and concise?

1. * **Social class** of the family that raised you: a) working class (those who perform labor that does not require a college degree), b) middle class (those who perform labor that does require a college degree), and c) owning class (those whose income or wealth is based upon the profits of their business (and labor of their employees) and not their own labor. Thus if your parents owned a business but were required to work each day to keep the business going, they would not be considered a member of the owning class by this definition. On the other hand if your parents worked hard to create a business and now can live off the profits of the business they are members of the owning class even though initially they were in the working or middle class. It is possible too to mix the classes. For example a member of the owning class who does not have formal education *might* be considered to be a member of the owning and working classes? These categories are still admittedly vague and oversimplified—you can clarify these categories if you wish. I provide these definitions only as a crude framework to help you be as specific as you can.

2. * **Your work history** (so here you will want to discuss those jobs that have influenced your goals either negatively or positively). How has your work experience influenced your direction and goals?

3. **Education** (how has your experience in school affected your goals?)

4. **Gender** - the "rules" of how to *be* a "man" or a "woman" vary from culture to culture and across individuals as

well. For example, do you react differently to the following two statements? a) "I noticed that he was crying." b) "I noticed that she was crying." What "rules" or values do you follow consciously or unconsciously that determine *how you think and act* as a man or woman? Do these "rules" or values influence or affect your goals?

5. * **Race/ethnicity/culture**—does your ethnic background affect/influence your goals? Do you have certain freedoms or restrictions based on your race? Do you have certain personality traits based on your cultural background that affect and influence your goals?

6. **Special circumstances and/or physical characteristics/ abilit**ies—perhaps you have the ability to leap 300 feet upwards into the air. Does this special ability affect your goals?

7. * **Family**—families vary greatly and each family imparts overt and hidden values to you. How has your family affected your goals?

8. * **Peers/Peer Culture**—think of your closest friends (or, um, those whom you wish to be your closest friends . . .) what are their values? How have they affected your goals?

9. **Local history** (example - economic and political issues) and culture in the past 10—15 years—How has living in, say San Jose, affected your goals?

10. * **National/International historical events**—how have some of the trends (economic, political, entertainment, music, etc) of the past 10, 20 or 50 years affected your goals?

Be careful. I am not asking simply for the story of you or your family. Instead I am asking: how do these above factors combine to shape your goals (or lack of goals if this be the case)? In other words I am asking you to give a series of *suggestive causal explanations* for your goals.

Note: you are not required to reveal anything about yourself that you don't want to. This is not a paper to assist you with your personal issues, but it is a paper to give you a sense of your personal social-historical context and thus help you to gain deeper insight and awareness into some of the social forces that have shaped you.

This assignment appears to have multiple WTL and WID goals. There is an emphasis on not only using writing for self-understanding and self exploration, but also using writing to practice philosophical ways of thinking: analyzing "causal explanations" in writing that is "clear and concise."

Some of the self-reflective writing in WAC courses emphasized thinking metacognitively about rhetorical practices, and asked students to explain their rhetorical choices or reflect on their reasoning processes. One example comes from a reflective portfolio review in SOM310:

Write a 1 page review of the work in your Personal Portfolio. Describe what you did and what you learned. Explain the writing choices you made, the obstacles you encountered.

Tell how the assignments were relevant or not to your future career trajectory, and also tell whether/how writing this portfolio was a good experience for you.

A similar kind of meta-reflection was asked of students at the end of an essay for S49 Philosophy 4:

At the end of the paper discuss how well you think you reasoned and the strategies or methods that you used when reasoning. Why exactly you reason well or poorly? Where did you "find" your reasons? What did you base your reasons on? What sort of reasoning "tools" did you make use of? Note: I am deliberately being vague here because I want you to reflect, without any guidance from me, on your *style* of reasoning.

Whether WAC instructors assigned self-reflective writing to encourage students to make personal connections to disciplinary content, to think about professional goals, or to reflect on rhetorical choices, it's clear these instructors saw the value in writing to and about the self, and this value was made explicit to students. A passage from a self-evaluation assignment in ENST495: Senior Seminar in Environmental Studies speaks to the attitude of most WAC instructors: "This is your education, you must be an active participant in it, and it is only you who can determine its value to you, through self-evaluation and reflection."

WAC COURSE ASSIGNMENTS ARE OFTEN WRITTEN TO WIDER AUDIENCES BEYOND THE TEACHER

In addition to self-reflective writing assignments, WAC courses often asked students to look outward, toward audiences beyond the classroom. Some assignments asked students to do both things at once: to self-reflect while also considering a wider audience. The personal mission statement assignment from SOM310 that I mentioned in the previous section is an example of writing that is both self-reflective and focused on a wider audience. The assignment asked students to describe their experiences, their personal business values, and the various influences in their life. But it also asked students to "Identify the audience for this piece in the upper right hand corner of the essay (recruiter, grad. school, instructor, venture capitalist, group of employees or colleagues, etc.)." This assignment was part of a larger business portfolio assignment, designed to be used as students applied for jobs in the business world.

In SOM310, as in many of the WAC courses in my research, students are more often required to write for hypothetical professional audiences, in actual professional genres, than they are asked to write for the teacher-as-examiner. An international correspondence assignment is representative of the writing in SOM310:

INTERNATIONAL CORRESPONDENCE

In this assignment, you will work with your partner to write a letter of approach and/or inquiry to an imaginary international client, with whom you hope to do business. Your correspondence might involve exporting or importing a product for sale, or providing a service, or engaging in some other type of joint venture (e.g., overseas manufacturing).

After selecting your country you will need to conduct some research to discover what you can about the country's business practices and cultures. Next you will use that knowledge to try to determine what correspondence strategies are likely to be acceptable, and what strategies would likely persuade him or her to want to do business with you. If you can find samples of letters written by business people from that country, it will help you to write yours, because you will have actual formats to use. Sometimes samples are not available, however; and you may have to rely solely on the strategies you've uncovered in your research (but in a US format), to write your letter. *As you write your letter, record your reasons for making specific writing choices.*

Ex. "We opened with this kind of greeting in the first sentence, because in our research we discovered that business people in this country would prefer X."

- *Note that the memo presenting your reasons can earn more points than the letter itself, because it is in the memo that you show how you are adapting your letter; the memo explains what decisions you made about formatting, and writing strategy, and why you made them.*
- Your memo and letter should clearly demonstrate that you've conducted research in order to understand the country/culture of the contact person. Your memo also should indicate why you are attempting to write with cultural sensitivity, since theoretically, you and your partner could just hire a translator and not bother with learning much about the client.

This assignment has many of the features of writing to wider audiences that make these kinds of assignments so rhetorically rich. Assignments written to wider audiences are usually in a specific disciplinary or professional genre, and in this case students are even choosing a professional sub-genre (a letter of approach or a letter of inquiry) and seeking out models of that sub-genre ("If you can find samples of letters written by business people from that country, it will help you to write yours, because you will have actual formats to use").

Rhetorical strategies for wider-audience assignments are not tied to what will convince the teacher, but to what kinds of persuasion will be most effective for the particular audience. In the case of this international correspondence, cultural sensitivity is a must. The role of research in an assignment for a teacher audience might seem random to students ("find five sources" or "don't use Wikipedia"), but the role of research in wider-audience assignments has a stronger sense of purpose, as this international correspondence illustrates. Research is conducted "to discover what you can about the country's business practices and cultures." Students will then use that research "to try to determine what correspondence strategies are likely to be acceptable, and what strategies would likely persuade him or her to want to do business with you." In addition to having a hypothetical wider audience to write to, students imagine a role for themselves to play other than just novice students writing to an expert instructor. They must take on the additional role of a business professional, working in an international context.

Similar to SOM310, most of the assignments in Economics 101 are designed around hypothetical situations involving wider audiences. The major assignments for the course included a series of memos, each written to the same boss, as the course description explains:

> For the most part, your assignments are in the form of memos to your boss. Your boss is a busy woman who heads the US negotiating team on climate policy. This includes being in charge of further negotiations on the Kyoto protocol. Think of her as a former Stanford grad who majored in economics with a natural

science minor but who graduated 10 years ago and has forgotten many of the details.

Most of the wider-audience assignments in my study presented students with a fairly generic audience (the readers of a specific journal, a board of directors, a fellow scientist, etc.), but these economics assignments gave students a more detailed picture of their hypothetical audience, including her major, her minor, and her current grasp of science. All the memo assignments provided this kind of rich detail, evidenced in this sample of three of them:

Due April 28. Your boss asks you to clarify for her the significance of discounting to the US policy position on climate change. She has heard some argue for high discount rates, others for low discount rates. She has heard some speak of hyperbolic discounting and others of exponential discounting. Write her a memo to help clarify this issue for her, indicating how significant this issue is, particularly in terms of optimal levels of emission control in the present. Be sure to cite the literature as well as your own analysis of the problem. The marginal cost per word is zero up to 1000 words (excluding tables, footnotes and references).

Due May 5. Your boss asks you how important technological change is to greenhouse policy. Some constituents have been advocating strict carbon regulations in order to induce dramatic reductions in costs of controlling carbon, though the cost reductions will not be seen for several decades. Thus, eventually, carbon emissions will be dramatically reduced, primarily by making it very cheap to do so. Others have suggested that additional technological change brought on by strict carbon regulations is unlikely to make much difference in climate control costs over the next few decades. Your boss in confused and wants you to clear the air for her and advise her as to whether she should push for strict climate regulations in order to induce technological change.

Due May 12. Your boss has heard that there is a great deal of uncertainty about the damage from climate change. She is worried that your recommendations that only modest controls be adopted (in your memo of April 19) are driven by your assumptions about damage (which she reminds you was 1.33 percent of world GDP loss from a 3°C temperature rise). She has read that in Bill Nordhaus' survey of experts (discussed in his book), experts differed on their assessment of the consequences of a 3°C temperature rise. The median response was 1.9 percent of world GDP and the mean response was 2.9 percent. Some responses were clearly much higher (and much lower) than these. For larger temperature changes, the mean damage was 6.1 percent. All this is rather unsettling to your boss. She has been basing the administration's position on your recommendation that emissions should be about 9 percent lower than they otherwise would be. She is proposing supporting this with a global carbon tax. She is getting heat for this. She knows many people are saying the consequences of global warming may be very severe. She would like to know how much the policies she is suggesting for the very near term would be changed if you are wrong about the magnitude of damage. She wants to know the effect of different assumptions about damage on near-term emission control levels, as well as the effect on the carbon tax that she is pushing to implement the emission control policy.

Students completing these memos are presented with detailed rhetorical situations that make explicit connections to the kinds of work students might be doing after they graduate. In other WAC courses in my research, students wrote to hypothetical wider audiences of the *New England Journal of Medicine*, *The Sciences* journal, a corporate consulting client, parents of children in a hospital, a congressperson, the *St. Louis Post-Dispatch*, and a mutual fund manager.

WAC COURSE ASSIGNMENTS INCLUDE ALTERNATIVE, DISCIPLINE-SPECIFIC RESEARCHED WRITING PROJECTS, RATHER THAN MIDTERMS AND FINAL EXAMS

One-third of the 400 courses in my research used the lecture/exam model, but only a few of the WAC courses included an exam of any kind. Most of the WAC courses were designed around writing projects, with some type of extended researched writing as a culmination of the coursework. In his course description, the instructor of CLST11.01: Greek Civilization explicitly stated how a final research paper replaced what could have been a final exam:

> **Long Paper (35 percent):** In lieu of a final exam, students will select a topic (either their own, or one from the list provided) and write a term paper of 8–10 pages. This is a research paper and will require additional reading in both ancient and modern literature.

Almost all of the extended, researched writing in the WAC courses in my study resembled the "alternative" forms of research writing I discussed in chapter 3. As I previously summarized, Davis and Shadle (2000) contrast traditional, positivist research writing—with its emphasis on reporting the known—with alternative research writing, which values the creation of new knowledge, exploration, and originality. Nearly all of this writing in the WAC courses asked students to make arguments, conduct original research, and practice disciplinary genres and knowledge.

One example of disciplinary research writing comes from a research proposal assignment in BIO 310: Evolution. This proposal exactly mirrors the research of practicing biologists, as this excerpt from the assignment description illustrates:

RESEARCH PROPOSAL I

Your assignment is to write a proposal (a plan) to study an evolutionary question of your choice. In other words, assume you are a scientist interested in studying a certain aspect of evolution. Using the scientific method, you would come up with some observations that resulted in a question that could be explained by at least one hypothesis. The proposal will be written like a scientific paper, composed of the following sections: a) Introduction, b) Materials and Methods, c) Results, d) Discussion, and e) References. These sections roughly correspond to the scientific method in the following way: a) observations, questions and hypotheses are presented in the Introduction, b) the experimental design with predictions are included in the Materials and Methods, c) the results of the experiment are reported in the Results section, d) data interpretation (e.g., did results match predictions?, etc.) and conclusions (do you accept or reject the hypothesis?) are reported in the Discussion section.

Even in this brief excerpt, it's clear that students are going to be practicing the primary disciplinary genre (the scientific paper) and the primary approach to scientific research (testing hypotheses by designing experiments), but students have the freedom to choose a topic, and it is up to them to design the experiment.

The most impressive example of alternative, disciplinary researched writing in my study comes from SOM310: Management Communication. In a group project that culminated in a "corporate portfolio," students were immersed in the work of corporate professionals. The assignment description is lengthy, but I include it nearly in full to show just how extensive research projects can be in WAC courses:

CORPORATE PORTFOLIO—GROUP CONSULTING PROJECT

Corporate Portfolio Components

- Mission Statement
- Corporate Profile
- Consulting Report (with letter of transmittal, executive summary)
- Minutes of Meetings
- Additional Elements of the Assignment
- Team Presentation
- Evaluation Memo (A combined self-evaluation and performance appraisal)

Working in a group you will select one of the five international communication cases available at our website, read and discuss the case thoroughly, and take minutes of meetings. You'll begin to create your corporate portfolio by writing a corporate mission statement and corporate profile or image brochure, and you'll also begin to research the cross-cultural communication differences you uncover in your case. Next, you'll collaborate to write a consulting *report* (and continue to take minutes). Finally, you'll give a *videotaped presentation* to the "client," and evaluate the results of your efforts in a concluding memo. [For the sake of clarity, the Corporate Portfolio contents are described again below.]

The report must identify the international, cross-cultural communication problems in the case (supporting your conclusions with research), identify possible solutions to the primary problems (after comparing and contrasting the possibilities), and propose a solution to the appropriate audience (i.e., offer recommendations, and offer an implementation plan, and reasons). Throughout the report you demonstrate expertise by carefully documenting your sources.

The presentation must present your company, your research methods, your findings, your problem identification and recommendations, and your implementation plan—in brief—using visual aids and to a maximum of 30 minutes per team (average of 5–7 minutes per person, minimum 4 minutes per person). Note that class members will evaluate each team's performance for grading purposes, using a standard form (you will not evaluate your own team), so—*it is very important that everyone attend each and every class day during the team presentations.*

The Corporate Portfolio includes:

- corporate mission statement
- corporate profile, with position descriptions [or you may choose to do either a print or online image brochure.] The profile and/or printed brochure may be included in the team report as an appendix item.
- minutes of all of your group's meetings
- consulting report, with its letter of transmittal, cover page, executive summary, and appendices (reference list (APA style), corporate profile/brochure, materials you think would be useful for the client, etc.)
- research notes, edited drafts, copies of articles and research materials

Mission Statement

Read one or two annual reports and try to get a sense for what a corporate mission statement is really about. As a team, write a mission statement for the company/organization in your case. Try to include some sense of your consulting group's organizational values in this piece, and note that although it is very short, the corporate mission statement provides the vision, and sets the overall tone and direction for the company—presenting the corporate "ethos" or character to the world.

Corporate Profile

Read 2–3 company annual reports and note the sections where organizations present who they are and what they do (their position in their industry, their management, their employees, competitive strengths, goals, etc.). Build a corporate profile, or image brochure (print or online) for the organization you are creating. Your image brochure/profile should visually convey what your organization is all about, and it should include the organization name (and logo, if you design one), address, home page, industry, major products and/or services that the organization offers, or causes that it espouses, employee expertise, divisions, etc.

Attach to the profile or brochure a list of your group members' imaginary position titles and job descriptions ("Bios")

This profile/brochure could potentially be an attractive, marketing piece. Note that in real annual reports, the profile would either be part of the longer annual corporate report, or it would stand on its own as marketing literature—for sales or recruiting purposes. [Your team could create a company web page as the vehicle for the profile/brochure if you have the expertise on your team, as well as the time and the interest. Keep things in balance, though, so that you don't steal qualitatively from your overall portfolio.]

Group Consulting Report—Background Theory and Knowledge

Your group's consulting report is a kind of proposal. The body of your team's report may be 5–6 pages in length, not including front matter (letter of transmittal, executive summary, cover page, etc.), and back matter (reference list and appendices). Most proposals are short, but some are lengthy (especially technical proposals). You should integrate page design, typography, and graphical elements to help the reader see and grasp information more easily (e.g., headings, white space, charts, tables, pictures). [See the class handouts on writing letters of transmittal and executive summaries for more information about these common elements of reports.]

The students in SOM310 were not merely regurgitating information or summarizing prior research, but instead proposing a solution and making recommendations. These recommendations were made in the form of a consulting report, a specific professional genre with its own purposes, audiences, and conventions. This kind of alternative researched writing wasn't exclusive to the twelve WAC courses in my study. As I discussed in chapter 3, I was struck by the number of alternative research assignments in my collection as a whole. But, however common this type of writing might have been in all the courses in my research, it was the norm in the WAC courses.

DISCIPLINARY GENRES AND WAYS OF THINKING ARE MADE EXPLICIT IN WAC COURSE ASSIGNMENTS

One notable difference between the WAC courses in my research and the courses as a whole is the amount of explicit talk in the WAC courses about disciplinary genres and ways of thinking. WAC instructors not only assign genres that represent the work of disciplinary insiders, but their assignments explain why these genres are important and how they function rhetorically. In SOM310, for example, students write in letter and memo genres, and the instructor explained the differences between a letter and a memo, pointed out the many letter types, and encouraged students to seek out examples:

- Note that although each item in the list below is labeled "letter," the same tasks can be performed via memos. The primary difference is that memos are internal documents (unless they are e-mail memos, which blur the lines); we also expect memos to be more concise.
- International correspondence often varies from US formats.

solicitation letters
proposal letters
response letters
thank you letters
bid and quote letters
confirmations
explanation letters
notification letters
congratulations letters
announcements

complaint letters
recommendation letters
transmittal letters
fund-raising letters
job applications
letters to the editor
resignation letters

Consult your textbook or see your instructor for examples of letters and memos.

The SOM310 instructor provided even more detail about the genre and rhetorical situation in the assignment description for a business proposal:

Proposals take a variety of shapes, depending on audience, purpose, and the situation, but all proposals have key features in common.

- A proposal is written to persuade an audience to act favorably on a solution to a documented problem. Proposals can be solicited, or unsolicited.

- Proposals are created in highly interactive processes. *Usually the proposal writer(s) will interview the persons with authority in the problem domain—often more than once.* Frequently the client will provide data crucial to the writer (especially for feasibility), and this creates a special relationship between the client and the proposal writer—an obligation to maintain privacy, as well as trust.

- Proposals usually offer an executive summary that relates the contents of the report to follow, and proposals are constructed of "arguments" found in variously labeled sections of the report, depending on what phase of the proposal process is being presented. *Preliminary arguments* refer to the problem identification and description phases (e.g., background, methods or scope, including causal analysis, findings, etc.); *supporting arguments* refer to the solution identification, recommendations (including feasibility and benefits), and implementations phases, etc.

Unsolicited Proposals. You may have noticed that lighting in a particular location on campus is not adequate, resulting in a safety hazard. Or, you may have experienced a problem finding childcare. Or, there may be hazardous conditions in your work environment. In each of these cases, you would first investigate the problem, talk to affected parties, speak to the person or persons who can bring about improvement or change, and then deliver your proposal report or letter to the persons who can initiate the change process. (Many such proposals are delivered orally, rather than in writing.) People generally write proposals in order to gain approval for projects, solve community problems, improve existing conditions at work, or bring about needed changes in a company, organization, or institution.

Solicited Proposal. As a consultant called in to solve a business problem, you are expected to investigate the causes, interview the persons who have responsibility in the matter, and come up with a plan for solving the problem(s). The actual problems may not be identical with those identified by the client (clients may not know what is wrong), so you can take nothing for granted. After consulting and researching, you would either send your client a report or a proposal letter, or, as is more often the case, make a formal presentation—offering recommendations and an implementation plan. Your client can act to eliminate or reduce the problem, possibly by hiring you for the implementation of the solution. In such cases, you are writing a solicited proposal, for which you may be paid—or your efforts may be rolled into a second phase, in which you are paid for implementing the solution. The client in any case relies on your expertise to a great extent. Consulting and consultants' proposals require ethics, expertise, and credibility on the part of the consultant.

From the first sentence of this assignment, the instructor turned students' attention to "audience, purpose, and the situation"—the rhetorical rather than the formal aspects of genre. The process of composing the genre was explained, and emphasis was placed on the important role audience plays in this genre. In the explanation of unsolicited and solicited proposals, the emphasis was on genre as social action: writing proposals to "solve community problems" or "solve a business problem."

The assignments in SOM310 do a thorough job of demystifying genres for students, but in other WAC courses—even if the full social action of genre isn't detailed in the assignment—instructors attempt to place genres in some type of disciplinary context and contrast the assigned genre with other kinds of disciplinary writing, as was the case with a book review assignment in HIST3151: History of the British Isles.

GUIDELINES FOR A HISTORY BOOK REVIEW

A book review is different from other history papers in that it does not ask you personally to discuss what happened in the past; instead, it asks you to discuss what one specific author/historian has said about what happened in the past. A review tells the reader what the author's goal was in writing the book or article under consideration, and whether the author fulfilled that goal or not. A review also should effectively describe the material presented by the author to sustain his/her thesis. This entails some summary of the book's contents, but it also asks you to consider the following questions:

Why has the author written the material (e.g., propaganda, historical records, nostalgia, personal advancement)? Determining the author's purpose will often tell you something of the author's choice of approach and evidence.

Consider what new ideas the book or article gave you about the topic in question. Do these "new ideas" make

> you change your way of thinking about the topic? Where do you go from here?
>
> Ask yourself what information is missing from the book that you need to know to understand and criticize the author's argument. Is this "neglect" a fault of the author or the reader? Does the author assume too much?

In this assignment, the instructor teaches students a valuable lesson about writing in history: that all genres are not the same, and the approach you take as a writer and the questions you ask need to be adapted to the particular disciplinary genre. The question prompts listed in the assignment have less to do with formal conventions of the genre and more to do with ways of thinking in history.

In CLST11S.01: Greek Civilization and ENST495: Senior Seminar in Environmental Studies, the instructors make connections between the genre of the abstract and the social action of the discourse community. In the Greek civilization abstract assignment, the instructor explained where the writing of an abstract fits into the process of scholars, and where it might fit into the students' processes:

> Writing a complete, but concise description of your work is a necessary first step for individuals interested in pursuing their research, either for presentation at a conference or publication in a peer-reviewed journal. As students, this same exercise can aid you in the writing process itself; the Abstract is an opportunity for you to set down in one place your ideas, the evidence you have, and the conclusions you will draw.

The abstract in the environmental sciences course was part of a larger scientific research paper assignment, and this instructor discussed the nature of scientific inquiry, how that inquiry connects to the scientific paper genre, and why the abstract is such a crucial part of the scientific paper:

> A scientific paper . . . should reflect the application of the Scientific Method. Recall that the Scientific Method involves

asking questions, based on some initial set of observations. The creative scientist then proposes one or more hypotheses, and then proceeds to design and conduct experiments to test these hypotheses. A scientific paper should be well organized, normally including the sections listed below, which are clearly delineated by appropriate headings and sub-headings. The text books and journal articles you read could serve as role models for how you might organize your paper. For papers that will be published for other scientists to refer to, the title and abstract are very important. Other scientists will first notice your paper in the table of contents of a journal, and will be deciding on the basis of the title alone.

In assignments and course descriptions, the WAC instructors in my study consistently mentioned the ways professionals in their disciplines make meaning, interconnecting their course goals, writing assignments, and the work students will be doing after they graduate:

> The purpose of this seminar is to . . . prepare for career and post-graduate opportunities, and life as an environmentalist beyond Keene State College. Along the way, we hope to also further develop . . . your critical thinking abilities.

> All histiography grows out of the astute question.

> Mastering the use of economic thinking tools will provide you with powerful thought and analytical processes that will enable you to translate data into information required for answering questions and solving problems.

The final passage listed above is from Agricultural Economics 183, and it is worth quoting the beginning of this instructor's course description to emphasize the degree these WAC instructors saw writing as disciplinary thinking:

> This is a writing intensive, a thinking intensive, and a learning intensive course. Memorization of facts and definitions is a useless activity in this course. Students in this WI course are expected to able to effectively communicate to their readers their understanding of the functions and operations of the food marketing system via clearly written communications. EFFECTIVE COMMUNICATION REQUIRES EFFECTIVE THINKING. EFFECTIVE THINKING REQUIRES A THOROUGH UNDERSTANDING OF THE SUBJECT BEING DISCUSSED.

> Students will be provided opportunities to utilize the think-
> ing tools developed in class to solve problems related to why and
> how the agricultural marketing system operates. Understanding
> and developing the capacity to use these thinking tools cannot
> be accomplished by memorization. Memorization of formulas
> and definitions is a useless activity for this course and for future
> performance as a business professional.

This instructor's insistence that memorization of facts and definitions is a "useless activity" stands in contrast to many of the
courses in my research, since so many of them relied purely on
short-answer exams. The rationale this economics instructor provided for why he doesn't create assignments that require simply
memorization of facts—that rote memorization does not prepare
students for "future performance as a business professional"—is
an argument WAC workshop leaders can make to help persuade
faculty to assign disciplinary genres rather than exams.

WAC COURSE ASSIGNMENTS USUALLY REQUIRE DRAFTING, REVISING, AND PEER RESPONSE

Almost all twelve WAC courses in my research required drafts of
writing assignments for feedback from the instructor, asked students to participate in some form of peer response, requested
that students turn in drafts to a TA or adjunct tutor, or a com-
bination of all of them. In HIST100.81: Intolerance and the
Birth of Europe, the instructor mentioned in his course description that "Learning to write well is a life-long process," and he
emphasized this by allowing students to rewrite essays after they
were graded. He told his students, "I am always happy to look
at drafts and revisions," and required two conferences with the
instructor as well. Peer editing is a component of the course,
and, despite the language of "editing," the emphasis appears
to be on the quality of arguments in student drafts. In his peer
editing directions, he said, "You needn't worry about correcting
each other's grammar, but you should point out any weaknesses,
contradictions, or flaws you find in your peer's argument."
In addition to peer editing in class, the instructor informed

students that "peers are your greatest resource at Cornell. Ask a roommate to help you find the perfect word that's eluding you." He also reminded students that the writing center has tutors "who can help you develop your ideas and improve your drafts."

A similar revision process was required in Agricultural Economics 183. In his course description, the instructor informed students that "each paper will be submitted as a 'next-to-last draft' and then will be revised based on review comments made by the Teaching Assistant. The TA makes comments and suggestions but doesn't assign a grade on draft." A peer reviewer also looked at the draft and, as in HIST100.81, the feedback focused on content:

> The reviewer will point out communications problems and ask questions or write statements in the margin of the paper to give the author feedback regarding the effectiveness of the paper in responding to the assignment communications task. The role of the grader is to evaluate (1) how well did the author respond to the assignment and the suggestions and questions of the review, and (2) how effectively did the author respond to the communications assignment.

With built-in peer, instructor, and TA feedback, WAC courses like these are clearly designed using a constructivist model rather than a lecture/exam model. In W2000: Writing in the Business World, the emphasis on writing as a social process was made explicit in the course description. The instructor wrote, "I have designed this class so that classmates are encouraged to work together. You will be expected to draft, revise, and edit most assignments in small groups usually by email." Additionally, writing as process and writing as meaning-making were linked: "We use writing as thinking on paper. We use revision to formulate a message that is reader-based . . ..Writing is a process where we complete several drafts, pick them apart then revise them for clarity and polish." This emphasis on progressing from early drafts to a final, polished draft was echoed by the instructor of SOM310: Management Communication in a complaint letter assignment description. The instructor encouraged students to "Be creative and messy in the early draft stage—focus on strategy.

Bring later drafts of your letter(s) to the Writing Center and to class for peer edits, and *be sure to show your work to your instructor.*"

The instructor of SOM310 not only required an extensive revision process, but she also connected that process to strategies of composing in the business world. Using a specific business genre to encourage revision and feedback—the progress report—she was able to connect process to professionalism:

E-MAIL PROGRESS REPORT MEMO

Send your instructor an e-mail memo: *Progress Report on Career Interview and Research Report*

Using standard progress report format, write a concise memo to your instructor. That is, use "progress report" headings, within a memo format, but be brief). Your memo should make clear who you have decided to interview and why, where they work (industry, occupation, etc.), whether or not you have conducted the interview, what you have found out so far, and how far along you are in writing a summary report of the experience. It should also inform your instructor of any problems you have encountered, and especially any problems that your instructor might be able to help you resolve.

Your content should be organized using progress report headings and strategies. That is, you want to offer the reader an *overview* of the project you are working on (to remind the reader, who may be supervising several projects, which one you are charged with completing). Next you want to report on *progress made to date,* including mention of challenges or obstacles, and including letting the reader know if you need help with any part of the project, in terms of additional resources, etc. Finally, you want to let the reader know *what remains to be done* and your estimated date for completing the rest of the project. Common progress report headings usually offer some variation on the following: *Project Description, Work Completed, Work Remaining.*

SOM310, with its portfolio assessment, peer response, and progress reports, represents the emphasis WAC instructors place on revising that goes beyond word editing to make global content changes and develop arguments.

Martha Townsend argues, "the WI course requirement (as with WAC in general) has served as a powerful vehicle for expanding attention to student writing as well as for conducting faculty development" (Townsend 2001, 240). There is no doubt these WAC courses stand in contrast to the majority of courses in my study. They represent most of the self-reflection assignments in my research, and at the same time ask students to write for real and hypothetical audiences beyond the instructor. These WAC courses stand out, not just for their assignment of disciplinary genres rather than short-answer exams, but also for their explicit placement of these genres within the social context of the discipline. They ask students to engage in extensive composing processes of drafting, peer response, TA or adjunct tutoring response, and instructor response. These WAC courses, as I will argue more fully in chapter 6, stand out in my research as an argument for the value of WAC programs, and the transformative effects WAC initiatives—like writing-intensive courses or writing fellows programs—have on college instructors and on the literacy expectations placed on student writers. These twelve case studies add to prior research of the effectiveness of WAC initiatives (Beason and Darrow 1997; Hilgers, Hussey, and Stitt-Bergh 1999; Soliday 2011; Strachan 2008; Townsend 2001; Walvoord et al. 1997). As this prior research has found, and as is true in my study, where WAC has taken root, it has had a dramatic effect on instructor pedagogy.

6

IMPLICATIONS FOR TEACHERS, TUTORS, AND WAC PRACTITIONERS

This book has aimed to begin to address Chris Anson's call for more large-scale research into writing across the curriculum: research focused on "larger scale measures of belief and practice" (24) that will explore such questions as, "What does it mean to write in a particular academic discipline? How do the criteria for good writing differ among diverse disciplines? What sorts of instructional beliefs about writing do scholars in different academic disciplines hold?" (1988, 3). Other than a handful of researchers in the 1980s who conducted surveys or collected undergraduate assignments from faculty at a single institution or a small group of institutions (Bridgeman and Carlson 1984; Eblen 1983; Harris and Hult 1985; Horowitz 1986; Rose 1983), large-scale research into college writing that could serve as a complement to naturalistic studies has been lacking in the field of composition studies. Ethnographic, longitudinal studies—such as Marilyn Sternglass's (1997) *Time to Know Them*, Herrington and Curtis's (2000) *Persons in Process*, Lee Ann Caroll's (2002) *Rehearsing New Roles*, Anne Beaufort's (2007) *College Writing and Beyond*, and the studies conducted by Sommers and Saltz (2004) at Harvard and Fishman et al. (2005) at Stanford—are able to focus on the *why* and *how* behind the questions Anson raises, using information from classroom observation and interviews to find out why instructors assign certain genres of writing and how students interpret and respond to instructors' assignments. It's important to acknowledge that large-scale research like mine can only focus on the

DOI: 10.7330/9780874219401.c006

what of college writing: what writing is assigned, and what these writing assignments can tell us about the rhetorical situations, genres, and discourse communities of college writing.

Despite this inherent limit, my study aims to provide breadth to go with the depth found in naturalistic research: a panoramic shot of college writing in the United States, as represented by 100 institutions, 400 courses across disciplines, and 2,101 writing assignments. Gathering assignments from course websites allowed me, as a single researcher, to emulate the breadth of James Britton and his team's research in their seminal study of 2,122 pieces of student writing from 65 British secondary schools, reported in *The Development of Writing Abilities* (Britton et al. 1975, 11–18). None of the courses in this research were fully online, but most of them provided rich data in the form of writing assignment descriptions and ancillary material, such as grading rubrics, learning outcomes, writing guides, etc.

This book has addressed a number of research questions regarding writing across disciplines:

- What purposes are students asked to write for in different disciplines?
- What audiences are students asked to address? What role are they asked to play as writers? What role do instructors play as audience?
- What genres are students asked to write in? How do these genres vary from discipline to discipline and instructor to instructor? What is the rhetorical context for these genres?
- How do academic discourse communities differ? Is there a generalized definition of academic discourse that crosses disciplines?
- How do assignments vary across types of institutions, between upper and lower division courses, and between courses associated with a WAC program or initiative and those not connected to WAC?

This chapter summarizes the answers to these research questions. In addition to reviewing the major findings of the study, I discuss the implications of these findings for composition instructors, writing center tutors, and WAC theorists and practitioners. These findings will also be of interest to high school writing teachers hoping to provide students a bridge to college writing, and college faculty and administrators who are currently involved in—or interested in starting—a WAC initiative at their institution.

SUMMARY OF THE MAJOR FINDINGS

There were some definite and significant patterns across the 2,101writing assignments in this research, patterns that sometimes supported prior research, sometimes worked against prior research, and sometimes revealed new information about writing across the college curriculum. I review these findings in more detail in the section that follows, and use these findings to form hypotheses about college writing in the United States. I can't generalize from my sample to all college writing with statistical confidence, of course: as I mentioned in chapter 1, according to the National Center for Educational Statistics, there were approximately 4,300 degree-granting postsecondary institutions in the United States in 2006–2007—the time I was completing my research—and to generalize with a 95 percent confidence level and 5 percent CI (margin of error) a researcher would need to collect writing assignments from approximately 350 institutions. Although I won't make claims from my sample about all of college writing, my research allows me to make stronger hypotheses than research that only looks at a single institution or a handful of institutions, even if my study can't ultimately achieve statistical generalizability to the population as a whole.

A Majority of the Writing Assignments in the Study Presented Students with Limited Purposes, with Writing to Inform the Dominant Purpose and Writing for Expressive and Poetic Purposes Negligible

The most prominent pattern regarding the rhetorical situations of the assignments in my study was the limited purposes students were asked to write for. Sixty-six percent of the assignments had informative purposes, with an emphasis on informing the reader (almost always the expert instructor) about factual details from a lecture or readings. Although a significant amount of the writing in the study was exploratory in purpose (13 percent), poetic writing and expressive writing were almost non-existent. These distributions are similar across types of institutions and at the lower and upper divisions. I'd originally planned to investigate the differences in writing purposes among disciplines, introductory and upper-level courses, and different types of institutions, but I quickly realized that there were no significant differences. Sixty-four percent of upper-division writing was informative, with only 3 percent of writing expressive and 0.4 percent poetic. At the "elite" colleges in the study (institutions such as UC Berkeley, Duke, and Cornell), 69 percent of writing was to inform, while only 1 percent of writing had expressive or poetic purposes. At every type of institution and at each level—from community colleges to "elite" institutions, from introductory courses to senior seminars—writing to inform was the dominant purpose. These findings complicate the commonplace assumption in WAC research and theory that, in most colleges, students face more rhetorically complex writing tasks as they move from first-year to graduation. These assumptions may be true for institutions with a formal WAC program (as I discuss at the end of this section), but, at institutions that lack WAC initiatives and requirements, I would argue it is just as likely that students' writing is dominated by informative writing to the teacher-as-examiner throughout their entire college experience.

Typically the required information for assignments with informative purposes comes from lecture material or the textbook, rather than the students' own experiences, as the exam questions I cited in chapter 2 illustrate:

> In your textbook, Steven Smith describes three different roles legislators might play in representing their constituents. List and describe each of these three.

> Describe the major factors causing changes in food consumption (see Chpts. 1–4) and describe the marketing channel for a chosen commodity (see Chpt. 12).

> Explain the principles of government identified in the text and in class as characterizing our system under the constitution.

> From my outline on earthquakes, explain the "effects" of earthquakes.

Short-answer and essay exams made up 21 percent of the assignments in my study, and the majority of informative writing was for the teacher-as-examiner. Only 17 percent of transactional writing asked students to write for persuasive purposes, and for an audience other than the teacher-as-examiner.

Expressive and poetic writing was a rarity in my research, and just sixty-two of the assignments called for expressive writing, with most of these coming from courses connected to a WAC initiative. My research contains only nine assignments whose dominant aim was poetic. What was true of British and American secondary school writing in the research of Britton et al. (1975) and Applebee (1984) over thirty years ago appears to be true of college writing in America today: instructors rarely assign creative or personal writing.

Even Though the Majority of Writing Assignments in the Study Presented Students with Limited Rhetorical Situations, There Are a Significant Amount of Exploratory Assignments in the Exploratory Journal Genre

The dominance of informative writing—and the absence of expressive and poetic—is similar to the results of previous studies. However, my findings differed from prior research in the number of journaling assignments, which typically asked students to explore ideas for an audience beyond the self. Exploratory journals—and their computer age equivalent, the electronic discussion board—were a common phenomenon in the courses in my research. The following passages from journal assignments are representative of the exploratory writing in the study:

> The journal is a space for you to investigate your own thoughts, reactions, and feelings on particular art ideas and art works. I'm

asking you to make connections between what you are learning and what you have already experienced.

Logs are designed to keep you up to date with the readings, to stimulate class discussion, and to encourage you to think about the class materials as both psychological scholarship and as personally relevant.

Treat the e-mail messages as an opportunity to express freely your own thoughts, opinions, observations, and questions. You may also use them to float preliminary ideas for your essays. Because they are informal you needn't be overly concerned with structure, organization, and rhetorical polish.

Think of it as a conversation in writing, or as pre-talking analogous to the pre-writing you do for papers. Our goal is not to produce expertly crafted individual treatises, but to develop the ability to think, respond, and communicate through writing. Your contributions should be informal, spontaneous, informed, and impassioned.

Although my research did not include any personal diary journals, journals are more or less the only genre that allowed students to test ideas and take risks, use personal experiences, and respond to peers. Large scale research conducted in the 1980s did not reveal a significant percent of journal writing being assigned across the curriculum, and the panoramic view offered by this study allows us to hypothesize that journal writing has taken hold in college writing in the United States—a finding that will surely please the WTL pioneers of the early WAC movement.

A Majority of the Writing Assignments in the Study Presented Students with Limited Audiences, Namely Writing to the Teacher-as-Examiner

Given that writing to inform was the dominant purpose for the assignments in my study, and that most informative writing involves merely delivering information to the instructor, it's not surprising that 64 percent of the assignments were "student to examiner." Just as I was curious if upper-division courses required less informative writing than lower-division courses, I wondered if students wrote for audiences beyond the teacher—especially the teacher-as-examiner—as they moved from introductory to upper-division courses in their major. I instead found that, just as informative writing dominated all levels of instruction in my study, the predominant audience for the assignments at all levels of instruction was "student to examiner." In upper-division courses, 61 percent of writing had the audience of teacher-as-examiner. The prevalence of the examiner audience held across various types of institutions as well. The instructor played the examiner role in 64 percent of the "elite" college writing in my research.

As disappointing as it was to see 64 percent of the assignments written to the teacher-as-examiner, a more dramatic statistic is the fact that nearly one out of every three of those assignments *explicitly stated* that as their audience. The 29 percent of assignments that fall into this category roughly coincide with the percentage of short answer exams. Even in senior seminars, one-third of all assignments were to a stated audience of teacher-as-examiner. On a more hopeful note, the instructors who played a more dialogic role as audience tended to collect and respond to drafts of student writing, and 50 of the 400 instructors in my study collected at least one rough draft from students.

Instructors in the Study Assigned Diverse Genres, but the Short-Answer Exam Was the Dominant Genre

The purposes and audiences of the assignments in my research were often narrow, but the same was not true of the genres. I was impressed by the variety of genres I found, including lab reports, abstracts, literature reviews, business memos, book reviews, and annotated bibliographies. My research supports Elizabeth Wardle's assertion that "there are a tremendous diversity of activities within the university, and a tremendous number of genres mediating those activities" (Wardle 2009, 781). However, students taking the courses in my research faced a challenging paradox: they were assigned a variety of genres, but that variety was overshadowed by the utter dominance of the

short-answer exam. As I discussed in chapter 3, I was less interested in classifying and counting genres than analyzing the ways
genres function as social action in the context of the course and
discipline, especially considering how instructors' expectations
for similar genres differed widely from course to course and
discipline to discipline. However, I found it was the genre with
the least "social action" (Miller, 1994)—and the least diversity
of form and format—that dominated, with short-answer exams
making up a third of the genres in my research.

These short-answer exams were uniform across disciplines
in their conventions, almost always presenting students with
"fill-in-the-blank" questions that required minimal composing.
They were uniform in purpose as well, mostly asking students
to inform, and to do so using rhetorical strategies at low levels of abstraction on Bloom's (1956) taxonomy: strategies such
as "explaining," "describing," or "defining." The audience, of
course, was the expert teacher who already knew the correct
answer—the most pure form of the teacher-as-examiner. In
these short-answer exams, there was no explicit connection to
the ways of thinking and meaning-making of the discipline, or
to the real work of scholars or professionals in the field.

The Study Provides Further Evidence that the College "Research Paper" is Too Diverse to Classify as a Genre— The Majority of Researched Writing Assignments in the Study Were "Alternative" Rather Than "Modernist"

Even as I grew weary of encountering one exam after another
when I collected and analyzed my data, there was at least one
genre of college writing that presented me with a pleasant
surprise. The college "research paper," which was actually too
diverse in this study to classify as a true genre, was most often
"alternative" in form rather than "modernist," using Davis and
Shadle's (2000) terms. They describe the modernist research
paper as a "traditional" research paper: informative in purpose,
logical, thesis-driven, and objective. The purpose of a modernist
research paper is "not making knowledge so much as reporting

the known" (423). Alternative research writing values the creation of new knowledge, exploration, and originality, and is
often written in "poststructural" genres, such as ethnography
or hypertext.

Compositionists like Richard Larson (1982) and Davis and
Shadle have bemoaned the staying power of the traditional
research paper, so I fully expected the majority of the research
writing in my collection to fit Davis and Shadle's modernist category. I was surprised to find instead that the majority of them
were closer in spirit to alternative research writing. The following passages from various research projects are representative:

> As an integration course, cross-cultural psychology seeks to
> involve students in exploring the interrelationships between two
> or more disciplines. The purpose of the project is to help you
> do just that. The format of the project is open to your creative
> ideas as long as the project looks at culture from two or more
> disciplinary perspectives.

> There are two options for the final project, individual proj-
> ects that deepen your understanding of the social movement
> you have been analyzing in your class papers, and collective
> projects that examine a new case (either the World Trade
> Organization protest or the "death with dignity" movement)
> to broaden you understanding of the theoretical questions we
> have examined.

> The purpose of this paper is to stimulate your thinking about
> "social or distributive justice." You are to develop you own posi-
> tion on this topic. Specifically, what principles should guide gov-
> ernment in determining what to guarantee its citizens.

> You'll begin to create your corporate portfolio by writing a
> corporate mission statement and corporate profile or image bro-
> chure, and you'll also begin to research the cross-cultural com-
> munication differences you uncover in your case. Next, you'll
> collaborate to write a consulting report.

David Russell has claimed that "Faculty tend to stick to the
traditional classroom genres of essay (exam), research paper,
and canned lab report, which have often fossilized into sterile
exercise, divorced from the myriad dynamic activities of the

discipline" (Russell 2001, 287). His assertions may be true of essay exams and lab reports, but fossilization may not be the case for researched writing. The researched writing in my study presented students with rich social contexts and complex, discipline-specific ways of making knowledge. My study provides those who argue for alternative research writing formal and convincing evidence that the teaching of the traditional research paper will not serve students well when they encounter the more sophisticated kinds of research writing that will likely be required of them throughout the college curriculum.

The Writing Assignments in Each Discipline, and Even Each Course, Are So Rhetorically Diverse That We Should Think of Each College Course as Its Own Discourse Community

The disciplinary contexts of these research assignments speak to a paradox in my findings: that there are generic features of academic writing, but they are too broad to be useful except in the abstract. The writing assignments in each discipline, and even each course, are so rhetorically diverse that in a sense each course is its own discourse community. Literature reviews in education courses are much different than those in biology courses, and even assignments from two courses in the same sub-discipline may differ significantly. The kinds of evidence needed to make an argument in history are nothing like the evidence needed to make an argument in marketing, and rhetorical strategies associated with key verbs like "explain," "describe," or "compare" look different enough across disciplines that phrasing "describe" or "compare" in generic ways is at best misleading—a finding that provides additional evidence of problems with the modes-based approach in composition textbooks and courses.

Despite these differences, a kind of generic, archetypal structure appears again and again in my research, one that instructors simply refer to as the "formal essay." This almost templated form of essay writing is discussed in strikingly similar ways in assignments across the curriculum, as is evident in these passages from course assignments in history, religious studies, and sociology:

> Your paper should follow the conventions of formal essay writing. There should be an introductory paragraph stating the thesis or organizing principle of the paper, several paragraphs supporting the main idea in the introduction, and a concluding paragraph that sums up what has gone before.

> Each essay should have a solid thesis statement in the introduction, should follow formal essay guidelines (introduction, body, conclusion), and should be carefully written to avoid grammatical and spelling errors.

> In order to write a good essay you need to develop a thesis. The first paragraph briefly outlines the issue your paper addresses then presents a clearly formulated thesis statement. The final paragraph simply summarizes what you have demonstrated.

> In the introduction give the reader an overview of your essay, then in each paragraph address one of the main ideas included in the outline. In the conclusion remind the reader of how the ideas are related.

The "academic essay," as it's defined by many of the instructors in my study, is rhetorically narrow compared to the writing academics engage in for their own scholarly work. This formulaic academic essay stands in contrast to the rhetorically sophisticated research papers in my study.

The Majority of Instructors Focused Heavily on Grammatical Correctness in Their Writing Assignment Criteria, Even When They Claimed to Focus on Critical Thinking in Their Course Learning Outcomes

Although courses in my research are diverse in genre expectations, instructors in my research do share one concern. The majority of college instructors in every discipline focused heavily on grammatical correctness in their writing assignment criteria, even when they claimed to focus on critical thinking in their course learning outcomes. Based on their discussions of grading criteria, instructors devote as much time to formal correctness as they do talking about content, and often grammatical correctness was a baseline for acceptability. Although few of the instructors' syllabi and assignment descriptions were without at least a few typos or grammatical slips, many of them expected papers that were free of error, as these passages from syllabi and assignments illustrate:

> I will expect correct grammar and spelling as a baseline, and will not assign a grade to papers that do not meet this baseline. (You can resubmit these once you have fixed them, but they can only receive a minus)."

> At a minimum, your writing should be free of spelling errors and grammar errors.

> I expect good, coherent reports, free of spelling mistakes and grammatical errors. Please use the spelling checker that comes with your word processor! Even then, you must still proofread!

Although I do not have evidence of these instructors' responses to their student writing, one of the strongest patterns in my research was the expectation of perfect grammar, spelled out clearly in the syllabi and writing assignments.

Courses Connected to a WAC Initiative Presented Students with Diverse Rhetorical Situations, a Variety of Disciplinary and Professional Genres, Self-Reflective Assignments, and Peer- or Instructor-Reviewed Drafts

Many aspects of my findings reveal a picture of college writing in the United States that is nearly as rhetorically limited as the picture of secondary school writing revealed in the studies led by James Britton in England and Arthur Applebee in the United States (Applebee and Langer 1984; Britton et al. 1975). But the most pronounced and the most hopeful finding in my research points to the influence and importance of the WAC movement. The courses in my research connected to a WAC initiative presented students with diverse rhetorical situations, a variety of disciplinary and professional genres, and assignments that asked for self-reflection and required feedback from peers, the instructor, and/or the tutor during the composing process.

Although only a dozen of the 400 courses in my research were connected to a WAC initiative, these courses stood out dramatically from the courses as a whole.

In terms of quantitative comparisons, the numbers tell a definite story about the power of WAC. Only half of the transactional writing assigned in WAC courses was writing to inform, compared to 66 percent in the sample at large. Instructors in WAC courses assigned twice as much expressive writing as the instructors in my research as a whole. Sixty-four percent of the assignments in the overall sample had the audience of teacher-as-examiner, but 40 percent of WAC assignments were written for an examiner audience. Only 5 percent of the instructors in my research asked students to reflect on their learning in assignments written for the self, but 21 percent of the WAC instructors assigned self-reflective writing. WAC instructors were more than twice as likely to ask students to write for wider audiences, and they also assigned significantly more writing. The average number of assignments per course was 5.25, but the average number of assignments per WAC course was 8.7.

Instructors from courses connected to established WAC programs at institutions such as University of Missouri, Cornell, Duke, University of Minnesota, and Stanford asked students to write for the greatest variety of audiences in the greatest variety of genres; encouraged exploration and self-reflection; and taught writing as a social process through invention activities, peer response, instructor conferences, and "final" draft revision options. These instructors adopted common WAC pedagogical tools such as journals, grading rubrics, peer response, and portfolio assessments. WAC instructors made discourse community and genre expectations explicit to students, and connected writing assignments to course outcomes and the expectations of the workplace. A surface look at my findings may cause some to argue that the WAC movement has had only a minimal effect on college writing in the United States, with an increase in journal writing and more emphasis on writing as a process being the only differences from research done before the growth of the WAC movement. But a more accurate assessment of my findings is that, where WAC has become a formal part of the institution, it has had nothing short of a transformative effect on the purposes and audiences for writing assignments, the amount of writing assigned, and the way instructors initiate students to the genres and discourse communities of their disciplines.

IMPLICATIONS FOR WAC, WRITING CENTERS, AND FIRST-YEAR WRITING

In chapter 1, I emphasized the value of taking an integrative approach when considering the implications of composition research, and not looking through a single lens of either Writing to Learn (WTL) or Writing in the Disciplines (WID). My research has implications for both of the major approaches to WAC, but it also speaks to the value of an integrated approach, one that—like the instructors in the writing-intensive courses in my research—synthesizes the two approaches. In his chapter on WAC theory in *WAC for the New Millennium*, Chris Thaiss says, "I count it one of the failings of theory in recent years that our sense of the connectedness of 'writing to learn' / 'the expressive' / 'the informal' and of 'learning to write' / 'the transactional' / 'the formal' has been lost to some extent in the drive of some scholars to stress the distinctions between theories more than their connections" (Thaiss 2001, 87). I do not wish to further reinforce the distinctions between WTL and WID in the ways Thaiss is concerned about, and I consider WTL perspectives, WID perspectives, and perspectives that integrate the two as I discuss the implications of the research, highlighting six specific recommendations based on my results.

Recommendation #1: Given the Lack of Expressive and Poetic College Writing, WAC Faculty Development Efforts Should Integrate WTL and WID Approaches, Using the Genre of the Journal as a Point of Leverage

Both WTL and WID approaches are relevant in response to the limited rhetorical situations of most of the assignments in my collection. Just as Britton et al. (1975) bemoaned the lack of expressive and poetic writing in British secondary schools, and the rarity of writing for the self, WTL theorists would view my findings as further argument for the pressing need to make faculty outside of composition aware of the value of expressive and poetic writing. WID theorists would also bemoan the prevalence of informative writing to the teacher-as-examiner throughout my research. For WID theorists, this problem speaks less to the absence of expressive and poetic writing and more to a different pressing need: the need to make instructors in the disciplines more aware of the value of seeing students, not as empty vessels to be filled, but as disciplinary apprentices—the value of assigning writing that moves beyond informing toward making arguments, solving problems, and thinking critically about disciplinary issues.

In WAC workshops, we can integrate WTL and WID approaches in order to encourage faculty to reflect on the rhetorical situations they present to students, moving them beyond informative writing to the teacher-as-examiner. Mark Waldo (1996) argues for an inquiry-based approach to working with faculty across disciplines, one in which, rather than trying to sell faculty on our preconceived WTL pedagogies, we ask faculty to reflect on the goals, rhetorical situations, genres, and discourse communities of their courses, and think about ways that both WTL and WID strategies can help them further their own disciplinary learning outcomes. Waldo argues:

> Writing to learn and learning to write should be acknowledged as occurring together in any classroom which uses assignments, differing between disciplines in increasingly complex ways as students progress. Students have to write to learn and learn to write within their disciplines in order to join them—with all that means to developing the cognitive strategies specific to certain communities. (1996, 16)

Waldo recommends beginning WAC faculty development outreach by asking faculty to consider whether their assignments match their learning outcomes; this could certainly be a useful way to encourage instructors to broaden the rhetorical situations they ask students to write for. Waldo also recommends asking faculty to reflect on how they learned to write in their disciplines; if we ask for this kind of reflection we can have them consider the kinds of rhetorical situations that were most useful to them when they were students. We can also ask instructors how they use writing in their own lives, both personal and professional, and to consider if they are asking students to use writing for the same variety of purposes and audiences.

Yet another way we can encourage faculty to broaden their purposes and audiences draws on one of the early WAC movement genres that—if my research is evidence—many faculty are already using: the journal. We can encourage instructors to use journals, not only to ask students to explore the content of class readings, but also to explore personal experiences, metacognitively reflect on their own learning, and tap into their imagination and creativity. As we discuss the uses of journal writing in WAC workshops, we can provide models of journals with rhetorical purposes that vary from expressive to exploratory to poetic to informative to persuasive, with audiences of the self, peers, and the instructor.

Recommendation #2: College Composition Courses and Writing Centers Should Provide Space for Students to Write for Expressive and Poetic Purposes

If students are not often asked to write for expressive or poetic purposes in their college courses, and if they are not often asked to write to the self as audience, we can give students space for these purposes in composition courses and writing centers. In our composition courses, we can ask students to compose in a variety of rhetorical situations, such as imaginative writing and writing just for the self. The students in my research almost never had the opportunity to write in imaginative ways, and almost never wrote for the purpose of critical self-reflection. A first-year composition course presents us with an opportunity to give students space to practice these valuable kinds of rhetorical situations.

Many of the rhetorical situations presented in chapter 2 will be familiar to writing center tutors, and—in my own work as a tutor and then coordinator of a writing center—I've found that students rarely visit the writing center with self-reflective or poetic assignments. One of my goals as a tutor, then, is to encourage student writers to draw on more than just informative and persuasive purposes as they draft. I may ask students to engage in expressive writing to brainstorming topics or develop personal examples, even if the assignment itself is informative or persuasive. As a tutor, I work consciously to encourage meta-cognition in student writers, and present them with questions that encourage reflection on their own reading and compos-ing processes. As a writing center coordinator, I do my best to encourage students to bring in a variety of literacies to work on, from personal to academic to public. Even if the students at our institutions are asked to write for narrow literacies, we can open up our writing centers to multiple literacies (Neff 1994; Trimbur 2000).

Recommendation #3: WAC Programs Should Redouble Their Efforts to Work against the Lecture/Exam Model, Using the Research Paper as a Point of Leverage

Just as both WTL and WID theorists would want to work against the limited rhetorical situations instructors in my research often used in their writing assignments, these theorists would be troubled by the dominance of short-answer exams. From a WTL perspective, this emphasis on writing as regurgitating is quite the opposite of writing as a mode of learning; from a WID perspective, the exam is the genre that does the least to socialize students to disciplinary ways of thinking. The WAC movement, in both WTL and WID forms, has always focused on the importance of active learning, but based on my research I feel that WAC programs should redouble their efforts to work against the lecture/exam model. WAC practitioners can offer workshops, retreats, and seminars focused on such things as alternatives to exams, teaching using disciplinary genres, creative approaches to assigning writing in large classes, and sequencing assignments. Any of these topics would help instructors see the alternatives to the short-answer exam genre. WAC practitioners need to be equipped with strategies for helping instructors find alternative, disciplinary genres that meet the same learning objectives as short-answer exams, but provide richer social contexts.

Another point of leverage for encouraging instructors to move away from lecture/exam pedagogy is the genre of the research paper. If, as my study seems to indicate, the research paper is a popular kind of assignment across disciplines—and one that more often than not is used as a sophisticated tool for introducing students to the ways of thinking of the discipline—WAC workshops can make explicit contrasts between the kinds of learning and disciplinary socialization happening in researched writing, and the limited learning and socialization happening in short-answer exams. If instructors are assigning alternative rather than modernist research writing, we can use research genres as a point of leverage—a pedagogical strength that can be built upon. In my own WAC work, I've been using researched writing as a starting point in faculty discussions about writing assignments, focusing on ways instructors can make extended research projects more manageable in the hopes of discouraging instructors from dropping these kinds of assignments from their curriculum, in favor of the easier to assess short-answer exams.

Recommendation #4: To Best Prepare Students for Academic Writing, and Tutors for Helping Students with Academic Writing, Composition Courses and Writing Center Tutor-Training Courses Should Focus on Rhetorical Awareness, Especially Awareness of How Genres and Discourse Communities Function in Academic Contexts

Given that there are a wide variety of genres in my study—especially researched genres—how can we approach genre in first-year writing courses without overwhelming ourselves and our students? I believe the students in my research would benefit, not from a first-year composition course focused on particular genres, but rather a course focused on genre awareness. Students would be better prepared to face the writing assignments in my study if they knew what genres are, the ways genres are situated in specific discourse communities, how genres function in academic discourse, and what strategies experienced writers use when faced with the challenge of composing in new genres. Attempting to prepare students for the genres of academic discourse in a single composition course—or even in a series of composition courses—is impossible. But to ask students to reflect on their rhetorical choices as they compose in a variety of genres—or to ask students to begin to investigate the genres they will encounter in general education and their majors (through the technique of rhetorical analysis)—is, I think, a realistic and useful goal for first-year writing courses. Yvonne Merrill (2000) argues that rhetorical awareness is a "portable skill students can take with them from their composition course into their other writing situations at the university." Moreover, the teaching of rhetorical awareness in first-year writing is a focus of scholars interested in writing transfer (Beaufort 2007; Brent 2012; Nelms and Leathers Dively 2007; Nowacek 2011; Rounsaville, Goldberg, and Bawarshi 2008; Wardle 2007) and the Writing about Writing movement (Downs and Wardle 2007).

My research leads me to believe that a composition course focused on rhetorical awareness and "writing about writing" would better serve students than a course that reinforces the formulaic "academic essay" or asks students to practice modes of discourse like "explaining" or "defining" or "arguing," as if these rhetorical thinking strategies don't differ significantly from discipline to discipline and instructor to instructor. Even a course that uses one of the popular WAC textbooks might confuse students about how disciplines differ instead of provide them with the rhetorical savvy to move from course to course, since so many WAC textbooks present only belletristic essays on various disciplinary topics, as opposed to actual writing from the disciplines. I am not arguing that composition instructors, many of whom are unfamiliar with genres across disciplines, should ask students to compose in those genres. I agree with Wardle, who says "genres are context-specific and complex and cannot be easily or meaningfully mimicked outside their naturally occurring rhetorical situations and exigencies" (Wardle 2009, 767). This notion that genres must be taught in their social context is supported by genre theory and research (Bawarshi 2003; Bazerman 1988; Devitt 2008). Asking students to mimic disciplinary genres may not be appropriate in composition courses, but first-year composition *is* ideally positioned to provide students with the kind of rhetorical awareness they can apply any time they are confronted with an assignment that asks them to write in a new disciplinary genre.

Like composition instructors, writing center tutors also need to be sensitive to the variety of genres students will bring to their campus writing centers. There is ongoing debate in writing center scholarship regarding whether it's more advantageous to be a disciplinary insider (a "specialist" tutor) or whether the generalist tutor is preferable. In their study of specialist versus generalist tutors, Jean Kiedaisch and Sue Dinitz found the tutor's knowledge of how to think and write in the discipline was important, and that only specialist tutors worked well with students on a global level (1993). Kiedaisch and Dinitz argue, "students writing papers for upper-level courses would be best served by carefully trained tutors with knowledge of the disciplines" (1993, 72). In a similar study, Soven (2001) also found that "the knowledgeable tutor—that is, the tutor who is familiar with the subject matter of the course—more effectively communicates the various understandings of writing promoted by WAC than the generalist tutor" (212). Mark Waldo (1993) goes so far as to argue that writing centers should be staffed by professional tutors with BA degrees from various disciplines. However, other writing center scholars have argued for the value of the generalist tutor over the disciplinary tutor, primarily on the grounds that specialist tutors may be more directive, whereas generalist tutors are more likely to ask open-ended questions (Hubbuch 1988).

Based on the discipline-specific nature of the researched writing in my study, I would agree with Kiedaisch and Dinitz, Soven, and Waldo that specialist tutors would be better equipped to handle the variety of academic genres and complex research assignment students bring to the writing center. However, given the make-up of most writing center tutoring staffs, and the logistical complexities of matching the assignment's genre with the most qualified tutor, perhaps the focus of our efforts should be the tutor training course. Just as we might teach genre awareness in our first-year writing courses, we should talk about genre theory in our tutor training courses. In her essay "Addressing Genre in the Writing Center," Irene Clark argues, "Approaching writing in terms of genre has considerable potential for expanding writing center tutors' repertoire of pedagogical strategies, enabling students to respond more effectively and creatively to their writing assignments" (1999, 26). Kristin Walker argues that genre theory "provides 'generalists' and 'specialists' [tutors] with a tool to analyze discipline-specific discourse" (1998, 28). Tutors may sometimes lack the disciplinary expertise to have an "insider" understanding of every genre students will bring with them to the writing center, but they should be equipped with rhetorical strategies for understanding genres that they can then share with student writers. Popular tutor training manuals and edited collections lack a discussion of genre theory and tutoring for genre awareness. Given the sophisticated disciplinary contexts of the research writing I found in my study, and the diversity of genres in the courses that didn't focus on the lecture/exam model, writing center coordinators would be wise to devote at least some of their tutor training time to genre theory and practice.

If the disciplinary contexts of the research writing in my study are sophisticated, the nature of academic writing as a discourse community is even more complex. As a panoramic view of academic writing, my research provides further support for the argument that teaching a generic "academic discourse" in first-year composition courses is at best pandering to the most reductive notions instructors have of what academic writing can be, and at worst giving students the false notion that there are generic strategies they can use when confronted with a vast array of genres and discourse communities throughout college. If we talk about academic writing in generic ways—in WAC workshops or in writing center tutoring sessions—we also risk painting with too broad a brush. Although it's true that many of the instructors in my research talked about the "academic essay" (which requires a simple thesis, logical organization, and a formulaic introduction and conclusion), diverse disciplinary researched writing in diverse discourse community contexts was more common.

Faced with the paradox of both the persistence of the formulaic academic essay and the reality of the diversity of academic discourse communities, what can first-year writing teachers do to prepare students and help them gain a critical understanding of their initiation to academia? Just as I argue that teaching genre awareness in composition courses is more useful than teaching any specific genre, I feel my research indicates that teaching discourse community awareness is more important than introducing students to either our imagined notion of "the academic discourse community" or any one specific discourse community. What would benefit students, I believe, is to know: a) something about the concept of discourse community; b) that some teachers have a limited view of the academic discourse community, while others have an expansive view; c) students will be introduced to a variety of discourse communities in their college careers; d) some of the sociopolitical issues involved in the formation and reproduction of academic discourse communities; and e) some of the ways—however limited—that students can change discourse communities through their own agency as rhetors. As Patricia Linton et al. argue, ". . . even if 'all' that general composition courses can accomplish is to introduce students to formal differences in the writing characteristic of different disciplines, that introduction is nevertheless a crucial stage in their acquisition of disciplinary style" (1994, 64).

I discuss the idea of "discourse community" in my own composition courses, and I know what a difficult concept this can be for students. My research leads me to believe that ways of thinking and making knowledge are similar enough in broad discourse communities like the social sciences, the natural sciences, business, and the humanities that it's worthwhile to introduce students to these communities in composition courses. At the same time, we can try to make students aware of the fact that there are many more communities within these broader communities, and that even instructors in the same sub-discipline of a department may have different notions of what counts as knowledge in the discourse community, or which genres are most important. Based on my research, I believe it is critical that we teach students the importance of thinking of each of their courses as its own discourse community. As Lucille McCarthy argues, "Successful students are those who can, in their interactions with teachers during the semester, determine what constitutes appropriate texts in each classroom: the content, structures, language, ways of thinking, and types of evidence required in that discipline and by that teacher" (1987, 233).

The same kind of pedagogy I am arguing for in composition courses can be applied to tutoring in writing centers. In addition to drawing students' attention to places in assignments where teachers, explicitly or implicitly, discuss the discourse community context of the assignment, we can ask questions that force students to think about that context. This could mean questions about the wider social context of a genre; about what scientists, historians, or artists do and how they do it; or about the discourse community of the class itself. We can encourage student writers to be more conscious of how their initiation to academic discourse communities affects them, and how they can negotiate between their own agency as writers and the expectations of the communities they are entering. Nancy Grimm argues that this kind of critical self-reflection on the part of tutors and writers can help them think through the "consequences of resisting, negotiating, or accommodating the tacit cultural expectations of the assignment" (1999, 32).

On a much smaller and more pragmatic level, as we work with students on specific assignments in tutoring sessions, we must avoid relying too heavily on our preformed notions of academic writing. We should treat each genre students bring with them to the writing center—even one we think we already know well—as something that will require classroom context. When we see key verbs in assignments like "describe" or "analyze" or "compare," rather than defaulting to a generic notion of what these words mean, we should think about both the discourse community context and the individual instructor's expectations. This means reading assignment descriptions closely, and asking questions about the instructor and the course.

If we treat academic discourse communities with multiplicity in composition courses and writing centers, we should do the same in WAC workshops. Workshop activities that encourage instructors to think about the expectations of their discourse communities, and how to make those expectations explicit to students in their assignments and rubrics, will help work against generic notions of academic discourse. When I've asked faculty in my WAC workshops what their disciplines value, rarely do they mention grammatical correctness as one of the primary components of disciplinary meaning-making. Refocusing instructors' attention to the most important things students need to know and do in order to move from disciplinary novice to expert can highlight the difference between what instructors might be emphasizing in their grading rubrics (which is often grammatical correctness, if my study is any indication) and what is emphasized in composing in their discourse communities. When WAC practitioners work with individual faculty in workshops, seminars, or one-on-one consultations, they should always keep in mind that each course presents its own discourse community. There may be similar expectations across broader communities (the natural sciences, the social sciences, etc.) and within the same department, but, in the end, each course *is* its own discourse community, with its own expectations and genres.

Recommendation #5: Given the Complexities of Learning to Write across the Curriculum, a Single First-Year Composition Course is Not Adequate for Student Success; Institutions Should, at Minimum, Require a Second-Semester or Sophomore

Composition Course Focused on Introducing Students to Writing across Disciplines and General Education Writing Requirements

The idea that each course is its own discourse community certainly presents students with a difficult challenge as they move through general education courses and into their majors, a challenge voiced by Dave Garrison, the student Lucille McCarthy (1987) studied in "Stranger in Strange Lands," and the students in Marilyn Sternglass's (1997) longitudinal study of undergraduates at City College in New York. One final implication of my research, which struck me as I thought about the experiences of students in the courses I studied, is just how much patience, support, and practice these students will need throughout their careers as college writers. The students must compose successfully, each semester, dozens of different academic genres, to instructors with vastly different expectations for writing. Additionally, at the same time that they are faced with complex, discipline-specific research writing, they are frequently asked to merely memorize information and parrot it back to the instructor. From a developmental standpoint, the students are being pushed in opposite directions—asked to both leap forward in their cognitive growth and also pull backward toward writing as a mere transcribing of "facts" from lectures.

I believe my research presents an argument for specific kinds of support, so that students like the ones who took the courses in my study will be able to succeed. I believe these students would benefit from a composition course that helps them to both demystify and critique the many new academic experiences they are faced with in general education. This is not a course in paragraphs and sentences, or a course in the generic modes of discourse, or a course in forming and supporting a thesis, or a course in "the essay," or a course focused on any specific genres, or a "theme" course. What the students in my research would benefit from is a course that introduces them to the concepts of rhetorical situation, genre, and discourse community. A course that asks them to critically self-reflect on the ways their own literacies—and the literacies they are encountering in their courses—are situated. A course that asks them to both investigate their instructors' expectations and also critique them. In short, a course on academic "literacies," not a course focused on any single version of literacy.

Even more effective than a single course, I believe, would be two composition courses: one that helps students make the sudden and difficult transition to college writing, and one that helps them make the further transition to writing in general education and their chosen major. A sophomore composition course is ideally suited to introduce students to composing in broader academic disciplines (the social sciences, the natural sciences, etc.) and to ask students to begin to investigate the writing assigned in their chosen major (or a major they are interested in, for those that haven't yet chosen). Amy Devitt argues "we cannot possibly teach all of the specific academic genres that students may need in academia" (2009, 343). However, I'm not claiming that it's the composition instructor's responsibility to teach students how to write in their majors, or that composition instructors need to have expertise in the writing expectations of every discipline. What we as composition teachers can give students are frameworks for the analysis of any rhetorical situation. We can help them know which questions to ask when faced with a new context for writing, and we can make explicit the roles genre and discourse community play in academic discourse. This must go hand-in-hand with writing-rich general education experiences. Based on my research, I believe a writing-intensive general education experience can best be ensured by structured, systematic writing initiatives that include a substantial faculty development component.

Recommendation #6: WAC Programs Transform the Culture of Writing for Students and Faculty, and Any Institution that is Serious about Student Writing and Learning Should Support a Formal WAC Program

The implications of my research for student writing at the upper division are clear. Based on the comparisons between the

12 courses in my research connected to a WAC initiative and the 388 courses that were not, implementing some type of formal WAC initiative has become one of the best things a college can do to ensure upper division students will write frequently, will write for a variety of purposes and audiences in diverse genres, will revise and get feedback, and will use writing for reflecting on their learning. Given the richness of the discipline-specific writing in my research, I believe that WAC initiatives embedded in the major are more likely to prove effective. However, I can't make definitive arguments about what kinds of WAC initiatives are most effective (a writing intensive requirement, an adjunct tutoring program, a cross-disciplinary college writing unit, etc.) from twelve courses in my study. Suffice it to say that, no matter the type of WAC initiative, where WAC is systemic and part of an institution's culture, it transforms the pedagogy of teachers and the experiences of students, replacing the lecture model with an active learning model, and replacing short-answer exams with disciplinary and professional genres. My research adds further support to the body of evidence that immersing instructors in WAC faculty development will transform the culture of literacy across the curriculum (Beason and Darrow 1997; Hilgers, Hussey, and Stitt-Bergh 1999; Soliday 2011; Strachan 2008; Townsend 2001; Walvoord et al. 1997).

THE DISCOURSE FRAMEWORK AS A TOOL

As Stephen North (1987) points out, James Britton and his team of researchers created a discourse taxonomy for the purpose of analyzing and classifying discourse, not for the purpose of curriculum design. Instructors influenced by Britton et al.'s (1975) *The Development of Writing Abilities* began assigning expressive, poetic, and persuasive essays, but it was never Britton's intent for his taxonomy of purposes to become a basis for writing assignment genres. In the process of expanding Britton's taxonomy and creating a framework of rhetorical situation, genre, and discourse community, I was primarily interested, like Britton, in creating a more fulsome tool for analyzing academic discourse, and not necessarily a tool for curriculum design. However, because my framework captures composing purposes and considers genres and discourse communities, I feel that it can be used, not just as a tool for research and discourse analysis, but also as a way to think about curriculum design.

In my graduate composition teacher preparation courses, I use the framework as a way to help new writing teachers move beyond a "modes-based" or "aims-based" approach—the kinds of narrow-view approaches taken by many composition textbooks. I want future writing teachers to avoid conflating either rhetorical strategies (such as "defining," "comparing," or "explaining") or rhetorical purposes (like "informing" or "persuading") with genres. Other than in composition textbooks, I found no such thing as the "definition essay" or "persuasive essay" in actual writing assignments across the curriculum. There are, however, genres—repeated rhetorical situations that represent social actions. That said, I also want future writing teachers to question the value of teaching specific genres (say, the literature review or the case study) without consideration of the way these genres vary in different discourse communities. The framework of rhetorical situation, genre, and discourse community can help composition teachers imagine a more sophisticated curriculum, one that will help prepare students for the reality of the academic writing assignments they will encounter throughout college.

I have also used the framework in WAC workshops to help instructors in various disciplines rethink their curriculum. In a typical semester-long WAC seminar, for example, I might spend one full session discussing the notion of rhetorical situation. I ask instructors to consider if the purposes and audiences of their assignments connect to their course learning outcomes, and whether or not they are challenging students to write in a variety of rhetorical situations. I also ask them to take their current assignments and rethink the role students play or the audience students write to as a way of giving their assignments richer rhetorical contexts than novice students writing to expert examiner. We talk about the value of expressive and poetic writing, and consider ways these purposes may be integrated into their current course goals and assignments.

Then, I might spend the next session discussing the concept of genre and ask them to create lists of the most common genres in their disciplines. To further refine these lists for the purpose of assignment sequencing, I ask them if there are any genres in their list that often cluster together in the discipline or workplace. For example, rather than just assigning a generic research paper, instructors might create a cluster of disciplinary or workplace genres that can become a researched writing sequence of assignments, such as an annotated bibliography, a research proposal, a literature review, a research article, and a conference presentation. In another session, I build on the discussion of genre and review the ways that genres constitute discourse communities. I ask questions that prompt instructors to think of the ways of making meaning that are valued in the communities they belong to, and we discuss ways to make these discourse community expectations explicit to students. I also encourage them to think critically about their discourse communities, and to consider the social and political consequences of assimilation into academic discourse communities for themselves and for their students.

One final context in which my framework might be useful is writing center tutoring. I would argue that, just as composition instructors would best serve students if they moved beyond the teaching of modes or aims and integrated discussions of genre and discourse communities, writing center tutors would be more effective if they concentrated on more than the immediate rhetorical situation presented in assignments but also on the assignment genre and the discourse community the assignment is situated in. As I mentioned previously in this chapter, this does not mean a static and generic preconceived notion of the genres student writers bring to the writing center, or a set of preconceived assumptions about what it means to write in a specific discipline. Rather, I'm arguing for a framework of rhetorical situation, genre, and discourse community that is context-sensitive, focused as much on class and teacher-specific expectations

as more generalized genre or discourse community expectations. The kind of tutoring I am arguing for is question-focused
rather than knowledge-focused. Tutors who imagine academic
discourse through a framework of rhetorical situation, genre,
and discourse community will need to ask focused questions
about the assignment, the class, the instructor's expectations,
the student's experiences in their major, their discourse communities outside of school, and so on. Tutors might also use the
framework to help writers understand academic discourse, and
become better equipped to both integrate and challenge the
new languages of academic discourse communities.

FUTURE RESEARCH AND THE FUTURE OF WAC

One of the benefits of large-scale research into college writing
is that it allows us to chart broad patterns of growth, inertia, or
decline. Thanks to the large-scale surveys of college writing conducted in the 1980s (Bridgeman and Carlson 1984; Eblen 1983;
Harris and Hult 1985; Horowitz 1986; Rose 1983), I was able to
think about the ways instructors' expectations and assignments
changed in the last thirty years, and speculate on the influence
of the WAC movement in that time period. I hope that my study
can serve as a touchstone for future large-scale research, as a
way for future researchers to make comparisons between college writing at the time of their research and college writing
at the beginning of the twenty-first century. In the forty years
since James Britton and his research team's landmark study of
secondary school writing in England, research in genre and discourse studies helped me shape a more complex framework for
analyzing academic discourse than Britton et al.'s (1975) taxonomy of audience and purpose, and I expect future researchers
to develop ever more sophisticated frameworks that can help us
paint even richer large-scale portraits of writing in college.

I also hope that future researchers, whether they are inves-
tigating writing in the disciplines on a large scale or small, will
bear in mind the calls by McLeod and Miraglia (2001) and
Thaiss (2001) to take a more integrative approach to Writing

to Learn and Writing in the Disciplines. When we further investigate college writing, I hope we can both respect disciplinary values and give ourselves space to critique those values. As theorists, we can see the value of expressive and poetic writing, even if we are operating within a social constructivist paradigm. When we consider the implications of research into college writing, we can integrate WTL and WID approaches in order to strengthen WAC practice.

One final direction we can take in our research is to focus more closely on the results of WAC initiatives. Based on the results of my research, and prior research into writing intensive courses by Beason and Darrow (1997); Hilgers, Hussey, and Stitt-Bergh (1999); Soliday (2011); Strachan (2008); and Walvoord and McCarthy (1991), we have evidence of the effectiveness of WAC initiatives, and we need to continue to collect this kind of evidence for the sake of WAC's survival. WAC program leaders need to also be WAC researchers, collecting quantitative and qualitative data about university writing initiatives, not just for the sake of their own program's survival, but for the sake of the WAC movement as a whole. My research illustrates the stark contrast between the writing assigned at colleges that don't have formal WAC initiatives, compared to writing assignments at colleges where WAC has reached maturity, in the form of systemic university programs and extensive faculty development. We need to persuade provosts, deans, and faculty senates that every college should have a WAC program, and that these programs need time to grow and truly take root. We need carefully sequenced university writing programs, from the first semester to general education to writing in the major, with plenty of faculty development opportunities and options for students to seek out support in a university writing center and/or tutoring within departments or writing-intensive classes.

My research speaks to the value of continuing to push for WAC programs, and the value of WAC as a reform movement. In his history of writing in academic disciplines, David Russell says: "From very early in the history of mass education, writing was primarily thought of as a way to examine students, not to teach them, as a means of demonstrating knowledge rather than of acquiring it" (1991, 6). If my research is any indication, this may still be true of the majority of instructors today. By implementing WAC programs, we are implementing reforms to the lecture/exam model and helping instructors move beyond the short-answer exam genre. WAC initiatives encourage instructors to assign diverse disciplinary genres, to assign writing as a social process, to ask students to reflect on their learning, and to make explicit the value of academic discourse communities. There is still work to be done to make college writing about teaching rather than examining. The WAC movement provides our best hope of making that important transformation.

APPENDIX A
INSTITUTIONS SURVEYED

DOCTORAL/RESEARCH UNIVERSITIES

Columbia University (New York)
Cornell University (New York)
Duke University (North Carolina)
Florida State University
Kansas State University
Montana State University, Bozeman
New Mexico State University
Stanford University (California)
University of Alabama
University of California, Berkeley
University of Florida
University of Hawaii
University of Idaho
University of Indiana at Bloomington
University of Massachusetts
University of Minnesota
University of Mississippi
University of Missouri, Columbia
University of Nebraska
University of Nevada, Reno
University of North Dakota
University of Pittsburgh
University of Rhode Island
University of South Dakota
University of Tennessee

DOI: 10.7330/9780874219401.c007

MASTER'S COMPREHENSIVE COLLEGES

Alaska Pacific University
Arkansas State University
Bridgewater State College (Massachusetts)
California State University, Sacramento
Cameron University (Oklahoma)
Centenary College (Louisiana)
Central Connecticut State University
College of Charleston (South Carolina)
Cumberland College (Kentucky)
Eastern Connecticut State University
Framingham State College (Massachusetts)
Keene State College (New Hampshire)
Lynchburg College (Virginia)
Manhattan College (New York)
Mansfield University (Pennsylvania)
Philadelphia University (Pennsylvania)
Rhode Island College
Saint Cloud State University (Minnesota)
Salem State College (Massachusettes)
Slippery Rock University (Pennsylvania)
Sonoma State University (California)
Southern Arkansas University
SUNY Oneonta (New York)
Tusculum College (Tennessee)
Walla Walla College (Washington)

BACCALAUREATE COLLEGES

Albion College (Michigan)
Allegheny College (Pennsylvania)
Amherst College (Massachusetts)
Bates College (Maine)
Beloit College (Wisconsin)
Claremont McKenna College (California)
Davidson College (North Carolina)
Felician College (New Jersey)

Fort Lewis College (Colorado)
Grinnell College (Iowa)
Kalamazoo College (Michigan)
Lafayette College (Pennsylvania)
Linfield College (Oregon)
Luther College (Iowa)
Macalester College (Minnesota)
Metropolitan State College of Denver (Colorado)
Middlebury College (Vermont)
Oberlin College (Ohio)
Pomona College (California)
Reed (Oregon)
Rocky Mountain College (Montana)
Sarah Lawrence College (New York)
Shorter College (Georgia)
Washington and Lee (Virginia)
Wesleyan College (Georgia)

A.A. COLLEGES

Austin CC (Texas)
Bellevue CC (Washington)
Blue Ridge CC (Virginia)
Cabrillo College (California)
Carroll CC (Maryland)
Casper College (Wyoming)
Cochise CC (Arizona)
College of Southern Idaho
College of the Sequoias (California)
Clinton CC (New York)
DeAnza College (California)
Edison CC (Florida)
Harper College (Illinois)
Kent State University, Tuscarawas (Ohio)
Los Angeles Mission College (California)
Illinois Valley CC
McHenry County College (Illinois)

Merrit College (California)
Montgomery County CC (Pennsylvania)
Murray State College (Oklahoma)
North Seattle CC (Washington)
Pasco-Hernando CC (Florida)
Tarrant County College (Texas)
Utah State University Eastern
Western Nevada CC

APPENDIX B
SAMPLE CODED ASSIGNMENTS

ASSIGNMENT #1 (ECON101: THE ECONOMICS OF CLIMATE CHANGE)

Purpose: Inform
Audience: Student to Examiner

Study Guide for Test 2

CHAPTER 4

Know how aerosols may provide a negative global-warming feedback mechanism.

Know how cloud formation may provide either a negative or a positive global-warming feedback mechanism.

How and why do the surface temperatures differ from temperatures measured by weather balloon and satellite?

How do current and recent temperatures compare to ancient temperatures?

Explain in about three sentences how mathematical models of earth's atmosphere work.

What predictions are made by mathematical models about earth's future temperature?

CHAPTER 5

What fuel(s) have the greatest proven and estimated reserves?

Under the Kyoto Protocol, how can parties reduce emissions of greenhouse gases?

DOI: 10.7330/9780874219401.c008

Define the terms nuclear fission and nuclear fusion. For what
are each of these types of reaction used?

ASSIGNMENT #2 (ENST495: SENIOR SEMINAR IN ENVIRONMENTAL STUDIES)

Purpose: Explore
Audience: Self

Learning Log

A Learning Log is more than a personal journal or documentation of work done, it is a tool to help you integrate your
thoughts on your course work, readings, research efforts and
personal experiences. This will hopefully help you clarify your
ideas and future goals through synthesizing your background.

Use your log to note progress on class assignments and your
project. Be sure to record your frustrations and failures, as well
as you successes. However, your Log should be more than just a
listing of the activities attempted or accomplished, it should also
document your ideas, thoughts, frustrations, reactions to events.
Furthermore, it should cover much more than just your project.
Comment in your log on class discussions, readings and other
assignments. Write about your views on environmental issues.
Jot down notes about future career and personal objectives in
the environmental field.

ASSIGNMENT #3 (MGMT201: PRINCIPLES OF MANAGEMENT)

Purpose: Persuade
Audience: Wider Audience, Informed

Voluntary Affirmative Action

You are the human resource manager at Thompson Electronics, a leading Silicon Valley technology software manufacturer.

In proper memo format, write a memorandum to Lauren Thompson, the CEO of Thompson, in support of a voluntary affirmative action plan. In your memorandum, clearly discuss what affirmative action is, how it might be implemented, and the benefits that Thompson Electronics could expect from such a plan. Spelling, grammar, and clarity will contribute to your grade on this assignment.

ASSIGNMENT #4 (ANTHROPOLOGY 8: ANTHROPOLOGY OF RELIGION)

Purpose: Inform
Audience: Student to Instructor (General)

Ethnography

Ethnography is the work of describing a culture. The essential core of this activity aims to understand another way of life from the "native" point of view. The first step of an ethnography is deciding what to study. Choose a social event or a situation that you would like to know more about and can observe in a reasonable amount of time. It is easier for anthropologists to study cultures other than their own, so try to find something relatively foreign to your own lifestyle and experience.

The second step of an ethnography involves thinking about the kinds of questions you would like to answer. Questions may be broad (Why do you do this? How do you do this?) or they may be focused (Why do people dress this way?). Research questions may change while you are doing fieldwork and you may not even know what they are until you are well into the process of collecting data, but it is important to remember that ethnographies tell the reader something about cultural values.

The third step involves choosing your research methods. For this course, all ethnographies must be based upon participant-observation and interview; other methods may only be used as a supplement to data collected by participant-observation. Like other anthropologists, you will learn about culture by doing what the "natives" do.

The final paper should include an introduction, a discussion of your research methods, a detailed written description of the "culture," and a conclusion that tells the reader what you have learned about "native" beliefs, values or behaviors. The major portion of your paper (6–8 pages) will be descriptive but your conclusions are very important for it is in this section that you will present a cultural analysis and tell the reader what you have learned from your research.

REFERENCES

Anson, C. 1993. "Chapter 1: The Future of Writing across the Curriculum: Consensus and Research." In *Writing across the Curriculum: An Annotated Bibliography*. London: Greenwood Press.

Anson, C. 1988. "Toward a Multidimensional Model of Writing in the Academic Disciplines." In *Advances in Writing Research*, Volume 2: *Writing in Academic Disciplines*, edited by D. Joliffe, 1–33. Norwood, NJ: Ablex.

Applebee, A., and J. Langer. 1984. *Contexts for Learning to Write: Studies of Secondary School Instruction*. New Jersey: Ablex.

Applebee, A., F. Lehr, and A. Auten. 1981. "Learning to Write in the Secondary School: How and Where." *English Journal* 70 (5): 78–82. http://dx.doi.org/10.2307/817387.

Bangert-Drowns, R., M. Hurley, and B. Wilkinson. 2004. "The Effects of School-Based Writing-to-Learn Interventions on Academic Achievement: A Meta-Analysis." *Review of Educational Research* 74 (1): 29–58. http://dx.doi.org/10.3102/00346543074001029.

Bartholomae, D. 1983. "Writing Assignments: Where Writing Begins." In *FFORUM: Essays on the Theory and Practice of Teaching Writing*, ed. P. Stock, 300–312. New Jersey: Boyton/Cook.

Bartholomae, D. 1986. "Inventing the University." *Journal of Basic Writing* 5:4–23.

Bawarshi, A. 2000. "The Genre Function." *College English* 62 (3): 335–60. http://dx.doi.org/10.2307/378935.

Bawarshi, A. 2003. *Genre and the Invention of the Writer: Reconsidering the Place of Invention in Composition*. Logan. Utah State University Press.

Bazerman, C. 1988. *Shaping Written Knowledge: The Genre and Activity of the Experimental Article in Science*. Madison: University of Wisconsin Press.

Bazerman, C., and A. Paradis. 1991. *Textual Dynamics of the Professions*. Madison: University of Wisconsin Press.

Bean, J. 2011. *Engaging Ideas: The Professor's Guide to Integrating Writing, Critical Thinking, and Active Learning in the Classroom*. San Francsico. Jossey-Bass.

Beason, L., and L. Darrow. 1997. "Listening as Assessment: How Students and Teachers Evaluate WAC." In *Assessing Writing across the Curriculum*, ed. K.B. Yancey and B. Huot, 97–121. Greenwich: Ablex.

Beaufort, A. 2007. *College Writing and Beyond: A New Framework for University Writing Instruction*. Logan. Utah State University Press.

Beaufort, A. 2012. "Review: The Matter of Assignments in Writing Classes and Beyond." *College English* 74 (5): 477–85.

Berkenkotter, C., and T. Huckin. 1994. *Genre Knowledge in Disciplinary Communication*. Mahwah, NJ: Routledge.

Bloom, B., M. D. Engelhart, E. J. Furst, W. H. Hill, and D. R. Krathwohl. 1956. *Taxonomy of Educational Objectives: The Classification of Educational Goals*. New York: D. McKay Co.

DOI: 10.7330/9780874219401.c009

Brent, D. 2012. "Crossing Boundaries: Co-op Students Relearning to Write." *College Composition and Communication* 63 (4): 558–92.

Bridgeman, B., and S. Carlson. 1984. "Survey of Academic Writing Tasks." *Written Communication* 1 (2): 247–80. http://dx.doi.org/10.1177/074108838400100 2004.

Britton, J., A. Burgess, N. Martin, A. McLeod, and R. Rosen. 1975. *The Development of Writing Abilities (11–18)*. London: Macmillan Education.

Burke, K. 1969. *A Rhetoric of Motives*. Berkeley: University of California Press.

Caroll, L. 2002. *Rehearsing New Roles: How College Students Develop as Writers*. Carbondale: Southern Illinois University Press.

Carter, M. 2007. "Ways of Knowing, Doing, and Writing in the Disciplines." *College Composition and Communication* 58 (3): 385–418.

Clark, I. 1999. "Addressing Genre in the Writing Center." *Writing Center Journal* 20 (1): 7–31.

Coe, R. 2001. "The New Rhetoric of Genre: Writing Political Beliefs." In *Genre in the Classroom: Multiple Perspectives*, ed. A. Johns, 197–207. Mahwah: Routledge.

Connors, R. 1997. *Composition-Rhetoric: Backgrounds, Theory, and Pedagogy*. Pittsburgh: University of Pittsburgh Press.

Crusius, T. 1989. *Discourse: A Critique and Synthesis of the Major Theories*. New York: MLA.

Davis, R., and M. Shadle. 2000. "Building a Mystery: Alternative Research Writing and the Academic Act of Seeking." *College Composition and Communication* 51 (3): 417–46. http://dx.doi.org/10.2307/358743.

Devitt, A. 2008. *Writing Genres*. Carbondale: Southern Illinois University Press.

Devitt, A. 2009. "Teaching Critical Genre Awareness." In *Genre in a Changing World*, edited by C. Bazerman, C. Bonini, and D. Figueirido, 337–351. Fort Collins: The WAC Clearinghouse and Parlor Press. Retrieved from http://wac.colo state.edu/books/genre/.

Downs, D., and E. Wardle. 2007. "Teaching about Writing, Right Misconceptions: (RE)envisioning 'First-Year Composition' as 'Introduction to Writing Studies.'" *College Composition and Communication* 58 (4): 552–84.

Eblen, C. 1983. "Writing across the Curriculum: A Survey of University Faculty's Views and Classroom Practices." *Research in the Teaching of English* 17 (4): 343–8.

Emig, J. 1971. *The Composing Processes of Twelfth Graders*. Urbana, IL: NCTE.

Fishman, J., A. Lunsford, B. McGregor, and M. Otuteye. 2005. "Performing Writing, Performing Literacy." *College Composition and Communication* 57 (2): 224–52.

Freedman, A., and P. Medway. 1994. "Locating Genre Studies: Antecedents and Prospects." In *Genre and the New Rhetoric*, ed. A. Freedman and P. Medway, 1–20. London: Taylor and Francis.

Freire, P. 1970. *Pedagogy of the Oppressed*. New York: Herder and Herder.

Fulwiler, T., and A. Young, eds. 1982. *Language Connections: Writing and Reading across the Curriculum*. Urbana, IL: NCTE.

Geertz, C. 1973. *The Interpretation of Cultures*. New York: Basic Books.

Gill, J. 1996. "Another Look at WAC and the Writing Center." *Writing Center Journal* 16 (2): 164–79.

Graff, G., and C. Birkenstein. 2009. *They Say/I Say: The Moves that Matter in Academic Writing*. New York: Norton.

Grimm, N. 1999. *Good Intentions: Writing Center Work for Postmodern Times*. Portsmouth, NJ: Heinemann.

Harris, J. 1989. "The Idea of Community in the Study of Writing." *College Composition and Communication* 40 (1): 11–22. http://dx.doi.org/10.2307/358177.

Harris, J. 2006. *Rewriting: How to Do Things with Texts*. Logan. Utah State University Press.

Harris, J., and C. Hult. 1985. "Using a Survey of Writing Assignments to Make Informed Curricular Decisions." *WPA: Writing Program Administration* 8 (3): 7–14.

Haswell, R. 1991. *Gaining Ground in College Writing: Tales of Development and Interpretation*. Dallas: Southern Methodist University Press.

Herrington, A. 1985. "Writing in Academic Settings: A Study of the Contexts for Writing in Two College Chemical Engineering Courses." *Research in the Teaching of English* 19:331–59.

Herrington, A., and M. Curtis. 2000. *Persons in Process: Four Stories of Writing and Personal Development in College*. Urbana, IL: NCTE.

Hilgers, T., E. L. Hussey, and M. Stitt-Bergh. 1999. "'As You're Writing, You Have These Epiphanies': What College Students Say about Writing and Learning in Their Majors." *Written Communication* 16 (3): 317–53. http://dx.doi.org/10.1177/0741088399016003003.

Horowitz, D. 1986. "What Professors Actually Require: Academic Tasks for the ESL Classroom." *TESOL Quarterly* 20 (3): 445–62. http://dx.doi.org/10.2307/3586294.

Hubbuch, S. 1988. "A Tutor Needs to Know the Subject Matter to Help a Student with a Paper: ___Agree___Disagree___Not Sure." *Writing Center Journal* 8 (2): 23–31.

Jones, R., and J. Comprone. 1993. "Where Do We Go Next in Writing across the Curriculum?" *College Composition and Communication* 44 (1): 59–68. http://dx.doi.org/10.2307/358895.

Kiedaisch, J., and S. Dinitz. 1993. "Look Back and Say 'So What': The Limitations of the Generalist Tutor." *Writing Center Journal* 14 (1): 63–75.

Langer, J. A. 1992. "Speaking of Knowing: Conceptions of Understanding in Academic Disciplines." In *Research and Scholarship in Writing across the Disciplines*, ed. A. Herrington and C. Moran, 69–85. New York: Modern Language Association.

Larson, R. 1982. "The 'Research Paper' in the Writing Course: A Non-Form of Writing." *College English* 44 (8): 811–6. http://dx.doi.org/10.2307/377337.

LeCourt, D. 1996. "WAC as Critical Pedagogy: The Third Stage?" *JAC: A Journal of Composition Theory* 16(3): 389–405.

Linton, P., R. Maidgan, and S. Johnson. 1994. "Introducing Students to Disciplinary Genres: The Role of the General Composition Course." *Language and Learning Across the Disciplines* 1 (2): 63–78.

McCarthy, L.P. 1987. "A Stranger in Strange Lands: A College Student Writing across the Curriculum." *Research in the Teaching of English* 21 (3): 233–64.

McLeod, S., and E. Maimon. 2000. "Clearing the Air: WAC Myths and Realities." *College English* 62 (5): 573–83. http://dx.doi.org/10.2307/378962.

McLeod, S., and E. Miraglia. 2001. "Writing across the Curriculum in a Time of Change." In *WAC for the New Millennium: Strategies for Continuing Writing across the Curriculum Programs*, edited by S. McCleod, E. Miraglia, M. Soven, and C. Thaiss, 1–27. Urbana, IL: NCTE.

McLeod, S., E. Miraglia, M. Soven, and C. Thaiss, eds. 2001. *WAC for the New Millennium: Strategies for Continuing Writing across the Curriculum Programs.* Urbana, IL: NCTE.

Merrill, Y. 2000. "Anchoring WAC by Focusing on Rhetorical Analysis in First-Year Writing." *Language and Learning Across the Disciplines* 4 (1): 71–3.

Miller, C. 1994. "Genre as Social Action." In *Genre and the New Rhetoric*, ed. A. Freedman and P. Medway, 23–42. London: Taylor and Francis.

National Center for Education Statistics. 2012. "Fast Facts: Educational Institutions." http://nces.ed.gov/fastfacts/display.asp?id=84.

Neff, J. 1994. "Voices from the Writing Center: Risky Business/Safe Places." In *Colors of a Different Horse: Rethinking Creative Writing Theory and Pedagogy*, ed. S. Bishop and H. Ostrom, 198–201. Urbana, IL: NCTE.

Nelms, G., and R. Leathers Dively. 2007. "Perceived Roadblocks to Transferring Knowledge from First-Year Composition to Writing-Intensive Major Courses: A Pilot Study." *WPA: Writing Program Administration* 31 (1–2): 214–35.

North, S. 1987. *The Making of Knowledge in Composition: Portrait of an Emerging Field.* Portsmouth, NJ: Boyton/Cook.

Nowacek, R. 2011. *Agents of Integration: Understanding Transfer as a Rhetorical Act.* Carbondale: Southern Illinois University Press.

Pemberton, M. 1995. "Rethinking the WAC/Writing Center Connection." *Writing Center Journal* 15 (2): 116–33.

Prior, P. 1998. *Writing/Disciplinarity: A Sociohistoric Account of Literate Activity in the Academy.* Mahwah: Lawrence Erlbaum.

Rose, M. 1983. "Remedial Writing Courses: A Critique and a Proposal." *College English* 45 (2): 109–28. http://dx.doi.org/10.2307/377219.

Rounsaville, A., R. Goldberg, and A. Bawarshi. 2008. "From Incomes to Outcomes: FYW Students' Prior Genre Knowledge, Meta-Cognition, and the Question of Transfer." *WPA: Writing Program Administration* 32 (1): 97–112.

Russell, D. 1991. *Writing in the Academic Disciplines, 1870–1990: A Curricular History.* Carbondale: Southern Illinois University Press.

Russell, D. 2001. "Where do the Naturalistic Studies of WAC/WID Point?" In *WAC for the New Millennium*, ed. S. McCleod, E. Miraglia, M. Soven, and C. Thaiss, 259–298. Urbana, IL: NCTE.

Soliday, M. 2011. *Everyday Genres: Writing Assignments across the Disciplines.* Carbondale: Southern Illinois University Press.

Sommers, N., and L. Saltz. 2004. "The Novice as Expert: Writing the Freshman Year." *College Composition and Communication* 56 (1): 124–49. http://dx.doi.org/10.2307/4140684.

Soven, M. 2001. "Curriculum-Based Peer Tutors and WAC." In *WAC for the New Millennium*, ed. S. McCleod, and E. Miraglia, M. Soven, and C. Thaiss, 200–232. Urbana, IL: NCTE.

Sternglass, M. 1997. *Time to Know Them: A Longitudinal Study of Writing and Learning at the College Level.* Mahwah, NJ: Lawrence Erlbaum Associates.

Strachan, W. 2008. *Writing-Intensive: Becoming W-Faculty in a New Writing Curriculum.* Logan. Utah State University Press.

Sullivan, P., and H. Tinberg. 2006. *What Is "College-Level" Writing?* Urbana, IL: NCTE.

Swales, J. 1990. *Genre Analysis: English in Academic and Research Settings.* Cambridge: Cambridge University Press.

Tewksbury, B. 1996. "Teaching without Exams: The Challenges and Benefits." *Journal of Geoscience Education* 44 (4): 366–372.

Thaiss, C. 1998. *Harcourt Brace Guide to Writing across the Curriculum.* Fort Worth, TX: Harcourt Brace.

Thaiss, C. 2001. "Theory in WAC: Where Have We Been, Where Are We Going?" In *WAC for the New Millennium,* ed. S. McCleod, E. Miraglia, M. Soven, and C. Thaiss, 299–325. Urbana, IL: NCTE.

Thaiss, C., and T. Zawacki. 2006. *Engaged Writers and Dynamic Disciplines: Research on the Academic Writing Life.* Portsmouth, NH: Boynton/Cook.

Townsend, M. 2001. "Writing Intensive Courses and WAC." In *WAC for the New Millennium,* ed. S. McCleod, et al., 233–258. Urbana, IL: NCTE.

Trimbur, J. 2000. "Multiliteracies, Social Futures, and Writing Centers." *Writing Center Journal* 20 (2): 28–32.

University of Texas at Austin. 2013. "Web U.S. Higher Education." http://www.utexas.edu/world/univ/.

Waldo, M. 1993. "The Last Best Place for Writing across the Curriculum." *WPA: Writing Program Administration* 16 (3): 15–26.

Waldo, M. 1996. "Inquiry as a Non-Invasive Approach to Cross-Curricular Writing Consultancy." *Language and Learning Across the Disciplines* 1 (3): 6–22.

Waldo, M. 2003. *Demythologizing Language Difference in the Academy; Establishing Discipline-Based Writing Programs.* Mahwah: Lawrence Erlbaum Associates.

Walker, K. 1998. "The Debate over Generalist and Specialist Tutors: Genre Theory's Contribution." *Writing Center Journal* 18 (2): 27–47.

Walvoord, B., L. Hunt, H. Dowling Jr., and J. McMahon. 1997. *In the Long Run: A Study of Faculty in Three Writing-across-the-Curriculum Programs.* Urbana, IL: NCTE.

Walvoord, B., and L. McCarthy. 1991. *Thinking and Writing in College: A Naturalistic Study of Students in Four Disciplines.* Urbana, IL: NCTE.

Wardle, E. 2007. "Understanding Transfer from FYC: Preliminary Results of a Longitudinal Study." *WPA: Writing Program Administration* 31 (1–2): 65–85.

Wardle, E. 2009. "'Mutt Genres' and the Goal of FYC: Can We Help Students Write the Genres of the University?" *College Composition and Communication* 60 (4): 765–89.

Wilhoit, S. 2002. *The Allyn and Bacon Teaching Assistant's Handbook.* New York: Longman.

Young, A. 1982. "Considering Values: The Poetic Function of Language." In *Language Connections: Writing and Reading across the Curriculum,* ed. T. Fulwiler and A. Young, 77–97. Urbana, IL: NCTE.

INDEX